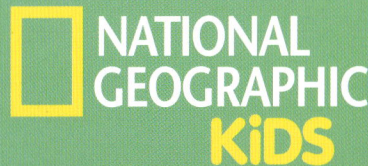

THE WORLD'S MOST AMAZING PLACES

Published by Collins
An imprint of HarperCollins Publishers
Westerhill Road
Bishopbriggs
Glasgow G64 2QT
www.harpercollins.co.uk

HarperCollins Publishers
1st Floor, Watermarque Building, Ringsend Road, Dublin 4, Ireland

In association with National Geographic Partners, LLC

NATIONAL GEOGRAPHIC and the Yellow Border Design are trademarks of the National Geographic Society, used under license.

First published 2021

Text copyright © 2021 HarperCollins Publishers. All Rights Reserved.
Design copyright © 2021 National Geographic Partners, LLC. All Rights Reserved.

Publisher: Michelle I'Anson
Project manager: Rachel Allegro
Text: Richard Happer
Typesetter: QBS
Proofreading: Tracey Cowell & Jon Goulding
Cover: Kevin Robbins

All rights reserved. No part of this publication may be reproduced, stored in a retrieval system, or transmitted, in any form or by any means, electronic, mechanical, photocopying, recording or otherwise without the prior permission in writing of the publisher and copyright owners.

The contents of this publication are believed correct at the time of printing. Nevertheless the publisher can accept no responsibility for errors or omissions, changes in the detail given or for any expense or loss thereby caused.

HarperCollins does not warrant that any website mentioned in this title will be provided uninterrupted, that any website will be error free, that defects will be corrected, or that the website or the server that makes it available are free of viruses or bugs. For full terms and conditions please refer to the site terms provided on the website.

A catalogue record for this book is available from the British Library

ISBN 9780008480134

10 9 8 7 6 5 4 3

Printed in India

If you would like to comment on any aspect of this book, please contact us at the above address or online: natgeokidsbooks.co.uk
collins.reference@harpercollins.co.uk

Paper from responsible sources

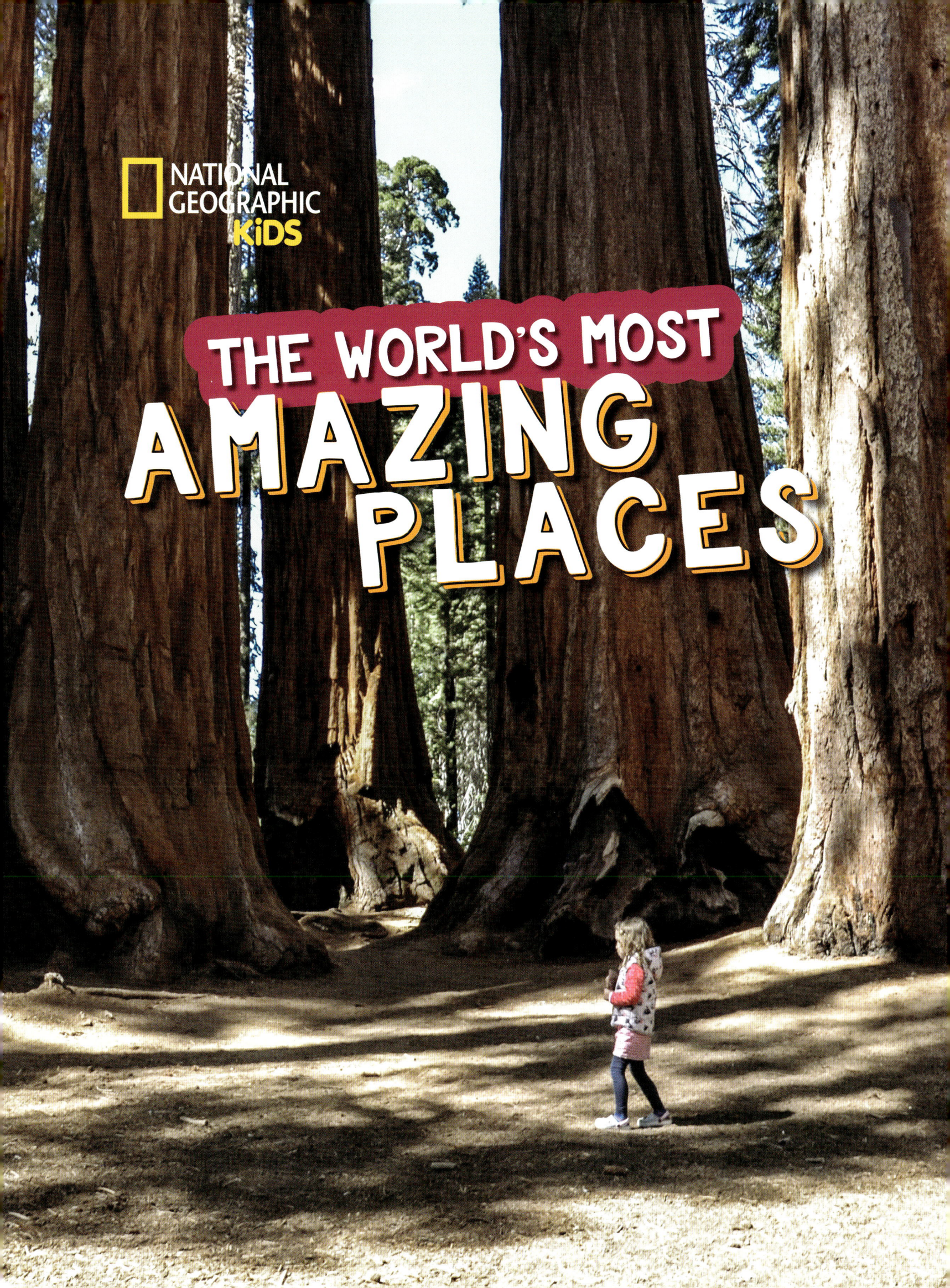

CONTENTS

OCEANIA
The Great Barrier Reef 8
Mariana Trench 10
Uluru 12
Te Wahipounamu 14
Shark Bay 16
Gondwana Rainforests of Australia 18
Komodo National Park 20
Tongariro National Park 22
Fraser Island 24

SOUTH AMERICA
Salar de Uyuni 28
Atacama Desert 30
Iguaçu National Park 32
Los Glaciares National Park 34
Angel Falls 36
Lençóis Maranhenses National Park 38
Caño Cristales 40
Galápagos Islands 42
Fernando de Noronha & Atol das Rocas 44
The Pantanal 46
The Amazon River 48
Huascarán National Park 50
Manu National Park 52

NORTH AMERICA
Cave of Crystals 56
Great Blue Hole 58
Talamanca Range – La Amistad Reserve 60
Death Valley 62
Hawaii Volcanoes National Park 64
Barringer Crater 66
Gros Morne National Park 68
Everglades National Park 70
Yellowstone National Park 72
Grand Canyon National Park 74
Great Smoky Mountains National Park 76
Kluane, Wrangell–St Elias and Glacier Bay 78
Ilulissat Icefjord 80
Dinosaur Provincial Park 82
Yosemite National Park 84
Monarch Butterfly Biosphere Reserve 86
Islands of the Gulf of California 88
Nahanni National Park 90
Carlsbad Caverns National Park 92
The Pitons 94

AFRICA
Kilimanjaro National Park 98
Victoria Falls 100

Whale Valley 102
Serengeti National Park 104
Lake Natron 106
Deadvlei 108
Rainforests of the Atsinanana 110
W-arly-Pendjari Area 112
Aldabra Atoll 114
Bwindi Impenetrable Forest 116
Danakil Depression 118
Virunga National Park 120
Okavango Delta 122
Tsingy de Bemaraha 124
Vallée de Mai Nature Reserve 126

EUROPE

St Kilda 130
Vatnajökull National Park 132
Norwegian Fjords 134
Danube Delta 136
Kvarken Archipelago 138
Mount Etna 140
Silfra Rift 142
Jurassic Coast 144
The Dolomites 146
Plitvice Lakes 148
Eisriesenwelt Ice Cave 150
Giant's Causeway 152
Wadden Sea 154
Aletsch Glacier 156
Primeval Beech Forests 158
Durmitor National Park 160
Western Caucasus 162
Doñana National Park 164
Virgin Komi Forests 166

MIDDLE EAST & ASIA

The Dead Sea 170
Lut Desert 172
Kali Gandaki Gorge 174
Pamukkale 176
Volcanoes of Kamchatka 178
Ha Long Bay 180
Rainbow Mountains 182
Wulingyuan 184
Lake Baikal 186
Hang Sơn Đoòng 188
Sichuan Giant Panda Sanctuaries 190
Great Himalayan National Park 192
The Sundarbans 194
Yakushima Island 196
Lorentz National Park 198
Red Beach 200
Lena Pillars 202
Kazakh Steppe 204
Ujung Kulon National Park 206
Nanda Devi and The Valley of Flowers 208

ISLANDS & OCEANS

Spitsbergen 212
Ring of Fire 214
Gough Island 216
Ross Island 218

Glossary 220
Index 222
Image credits 224

OCEANIA

Shark Bay

1. The Great Barrier Reef
2. Mariana Trench
3. Uluru
4. Te Wahipounamu
5. Shark Bay
6. Gondwana Rainforests of Australia
7. Komodo National Park
8. Tongariro National Park
9. Fraser Island

Uluru

THE GREAT BARRIER REEF

The Great Barrier Reef, off the eastern coast of Australia, is the largest living structure on Earth.

Of all the coral in the world, a third of it can be found here!

It is a huge coral reef ecosystem, home to hundreds of types of colourful coral and bursting with marine animals. WOW!

In total the Great Barrier Reef is made up of around 2,500 individual reefs and over 900 islands.

The reef stretches for over 2,300 km and covers an area about the size of Italy.

Beneath the surface, the reef is home to hard and soft corals, as well as amazingly-coloured fish, such as the stars of *Finding Nemo* — the stripy clownfish and bright blue surgeonfish.

Many types of sea snake weave their way around the reef. Even though most are venomous, they are fairly shy and unlikely to bite divers.

The reef is also home to many endangered species like the dugong (also known as 'sea cows') and green turtle.

Scientists have a lot to study on the Great Barrier Reef, and there are more than 60 reef-saving projects underway.

Global warming has caused sea temperatures to rise and this causes damage to the reef. Algae that live on the coral, and provide it with food, leave the warmer waters. The coral turns white giving it a 'bleached' look, and much of the reef is now dying.

Clownfish

MARIANA TRENCH

The Mariana Trench in the Western Pacific Ocean is the deepest part of the world's oceans.

It was formed 180 million years ago and is one of the oldest parts of the world's seabeds.

The trench is at a place where one tectonic plate (the vast rocky areas of the Earth's crust) is pushed beneath another.

It is more than 2,540 km long and around 69 km wide.

The very deepest part is called the Challenger Deep. The seabed here is nearly 11,000 metres below the surface.

The Challenger Deep was first discovered in 1875 by the research ship HMS Challenger, after which it is named.

If you put the world's highest mountain — Mount Everest — into the trench, its peak would still be two kilometres under water! WOW!

The pressure at the bottom of the trench is more than 1,071 times the pressure at the surface of the Earth. Anything that is not designed to survive high pressure will be crushed by the water. Anglerfish, certain jellyfish and translucent seapigs have all adapted to withstand the high pressure.

Living organisms have been found at a record depth of 10,600 m in the trench.

In 2012, the film director James Cameron went all the way to the bottom of the trench in a special underwater vehicle.

Anglerfish

OCEANIA

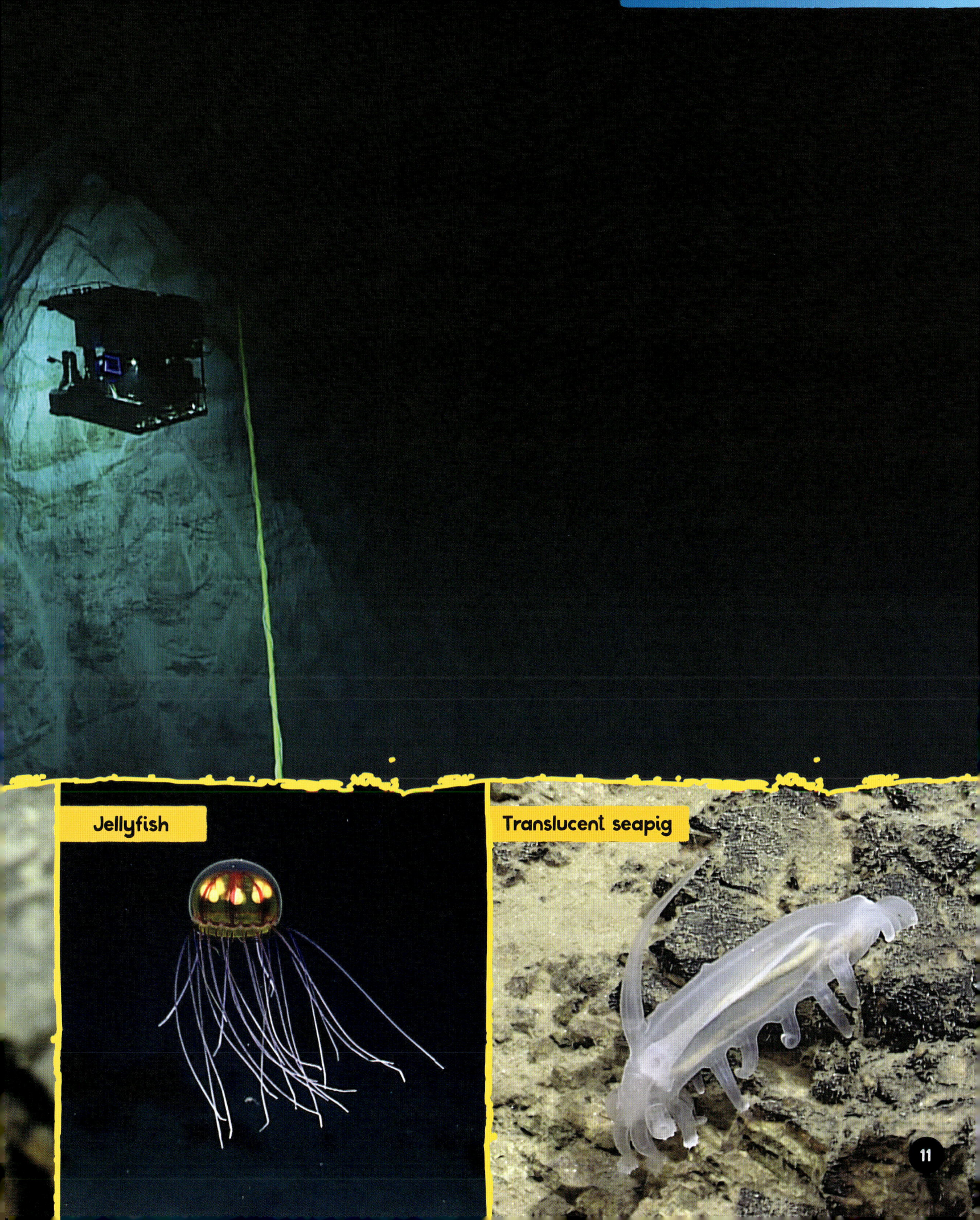

Jellyfish

Translucent seapig

ULURU

Uluru is one of the world's largest monoliths — a huge single rock standing on its own.

The rock was formed 550 million years ago.

Uluru is a famous natural landmark of Australia, and is also sometimes called Ayers Rock. Explorer William Gosse first saw the rock in 1873 and named it after South Australia's Premier at the time — Sir Henry Ayers.

Uluru is far away from towns and communities. The nearest town, Alice Springs, is 335 km away — a long way to walk for a pint of milk!

The rock is 348 m high, which makes it even taller than the Eiffel Tower.

Uluru is very special to the local native tribes — Aboriginal people — who believe that it is the resting place for ancient spirits.

The rock looks like it magically changes colour over the day. It can look dull brown in the morning, but often glows bright red at sunset. WOW!

Uluru is made of solid sandstone. Surprisingly, most of the rock lies under the ground, but no-one knows quite how deep it goes!

Lots of interesting animal species live nearby, like the wallaby, possum and bilby.

Many species of bat sleep in Uluru's cracks and caves, and they can be seen swooping around catching insects at dusk.

OCEANIA

TE WAHIPOUNAMU

COOL!

Te Wahipounamu on New Zealand's South Island is an incredibly varied **landscape**, with snow-capped peaks, sapphire lakes, waterfalls and fjords (deep, steep-sided valleys usually filled with sea water).

Te Wahipounamu means 'the place of greenstone' in the local Maori language.

Four separate national parks come together to form Te Wahipounamu. Together they make up 10% of the whole of New Zealand's land area.

Te Wahipounamu is home to Aoraki (also known as Mount Cook). It is 3,724 m high — almost four times the height of England's highest mountain, Scafell Pike — and is New Zealand's tallest mountain.

Hundreds of the world's most active glaciers can be found here.

Fox Glacier and Franz Josef Glacier are the area's main glaciers — they are both at least 12 km long.

The kakapo is the world's rarest and heaviest parrot — weighing in at about the same as a house cat! It once thrived in the forests here, but it may now sadly be extinct in the area.

Kiwi birds live in areas of Te Wahipounamu — they are a famous symbol of New Zealand. Interestingly, they can't fly!

Te Wahipounamu's Milford Sound is a beautiful fjord with very steep mountains rising from the inlet. It is also one of the wettest places in the world!

The area around Milford Sound is known for its ancient rainforest, which shows how plant life looked more than 180 million years ago.

Franz Josef Glacier

Kakapo

OCEANIA

Milford Sound

Rainforest at Milford Sound

SHARK BAY

Shark Bay is an amazing marine landscape and home to the oldest life-form on Earth.

Stromatolites live in the waters here. These micro-organisms (incredibly small creatures) are the **oldest form of life** on Earth – they are like **living fossils!**

The bay is at the most westerly point of Australia, where the land meets the Indian Ocean.

Shark Bay includes beaches, islands, inlets, cliffs and peninsulas – pieces of land that stick out into the water.

Seagrass grows in the shallow waters here. The bay has the largest bank of seagrass in the world.

The bay has a large numbers of dolphins, sharks, rays, turtles and fish.

At least 28 shark species swim here, including the huge, stripy tiger shark.

The bay is home to about 10,000 dugongs (also called 'sea cows') – 12.5% of the world's total population.

Clever bottlenose dolphins protect their nose with a sponge while looking for food in the sandy seabed.

The world's biggest fish, the whale shark, can be seen in the bay in April and May.

Tiger shark

OCEANIA

Tidal inlet

Bottlenose dolphins

GONDWANA
RAINFORESTS OF AUSTRALIA

The Gondwana Rainforests of Australia make up the **biggest subtropical rainforest** in the world. *WOW!*

Gondwana was a supercontinent (a huge area of land bigger than several countries) that existed over 180 million years ago.

The plates of the Earth's crust moved apart and Gondwana developed into the continents we have today.

Many of the plants and animals in these forests have their origins in Gondwana.

Rainforests are a safe place for many threatened species of plants and animals.

More than 200 rare plant and animal species live in the forests.

Animals that live here include wallabies, kangaroos, wombats, possums, koalas, echidnas and the sugar glider.

The Hastings river mouse and parma wallaby were thought to be extinct but were recently found living in these rainforests.

The Hastings river mouse has bulging eyes with black rings around them.

The rainforest is also home to half of all of Australia's types of plants!

Sugar glider

OCEANIA

Wombat

Parma wallaby

KOMODO NATIONAL PARK

Komodo National Park is a rugged coastal landscape on the Lesser Sunda Islands in Indonesia.

There are 3 large islands in the national park and 26 smaller ones, and it's home to the world's largest lizard — the Komodo dragon.

Komodo dragons can grow to be more than 3 m long and weigh over 70 kg.

WOW!

Komodo dragons mostly prey on a small species of deer native to the area — Timor deer.

These giant lizards sneak up on their prey and then attack, running at up to 20 km/h.

Komodo dragons also have venom glands full of toxins. When they bite their prey, it is injected with venom that sends it into shock.

There are many species of snakes on the islands, including cobras, pythons and vipers.

Banded sea kraits, venomous sea snakes, swim in the coastal waters around the park.

Large mammals in the park include water buffalo and the crab-eating macaque. Despite its name, the crab-eating macaque mainly eats fruits and seeds!

The park is also home to the white-bellied sea eagle and the very rare Flores hawk-eagle.

Komodo dragon

OCEANIA

Banded sea krait

Crab-eating macaque

TONGARIRO NATIONAL PARK

Tui

Tongariro National Park is the oldest national park in New Zealand. It is found in the central North Island and was set up in 1887.

In the heart of the park are three active volcanoes — Ruapehu, Ngauruhoe and Tongariro. COOL!

Mount Ruapehu is the largest active volcano in New Zealand, standing 2,797 m high.

Crater Lake is a deep crater on Ruapehu's summit plateau, which is filled with hot, acidic water.

Mount Ngauruhoe erupted 45 times in the 20th century, most recently in 1977.

It featured as Mount Doom in the *Lord of the Rings* films.

There are stunning emerald lakes in the craters near the summit of Mount Tongariro.

Many beautiful birds live in the national park, including blue ducks, North Island fernbirds, double-banded plovers, tuis, New Zealand bellbirds and grey warblers.

The North Island brown kiwi is common here. It can't fly and it holds the world record for laying the largest eggs relative to its body size.

There are two species of bats in the park. Bats are the only type of mammal native to New Zealand.

OCEANIA

Blue duck

North Island brown kiwi

FRASER ISLAND

At 122 km long, Fraser Island is the largest sand island in the world. It is found off Australia's eastern Queensland coast.

Fraser Island's sand-dunes, tropical rainforests, lakes and massive beaches make it a place unlike any other.

The island has more than 100 freshwater lakes, which are some of the cleanest in the world.

The island is made of drifting sand that has built up on a foundation of bedrock.

It has taken 750,000 years for the island to form.

Wild dingoes prowl along the island's sandy paths.

This is the only place on Earth where tall rainforest plants grow in sand.

COOL!

The King fern, which has the largest leaves in the world, grows on the island. Its leaves can be 9 m long!

Great white, bull and tiger sharks cruise around the waters surrounding the island.

Saltwater crocodiles can sometimes be seen snoozing in the shallows.

Wild dingo

OCEANIA

King fern

Bull shark

SOUTH AMERICA

Galápagos Islands

Angel Falls

The Pantanal

Los Glaciares National Park

1 Salar de Uyuni
2 Atacama Desert
3 Iguaçu National Park
4 Los Glaciares National Park
5 Angel Falls
6 Lençóis Maranhenses National Park
7 Caño Cristales
8 Galápagos Islands
9 Fernando de Noronha & Atol das Rocas
10 The Pantanal
11 The Amazon River
12 Huascarán National Park
13 Manu National Park

SALAR DE UYUNI

Salar de Uyuni is in the Andes mountains of Bolivia at a height of 3,656 metres.

It is the world's largest salt flat.

The salt flat is also known as a 'playa.'

The playa covers an area of **10,000 km²** — which is about half the size of Wales.

WOW!

The playa is incredibly flat — there is no more than 1 metre difference in height across its whole area.

As the playa is so flat and stable, it makes it ideal for checking that distance-measuring equipment in satellites is accurate.

Heavy rainfall can add a thin layer of still water to the playa that transforms the flat into the world's largest mirror!

Salar de Uyuni holds 10 billion tonnes of salt.

The conditions on the salt flat are so harsh that almost no plants or animals can survive there.

The salt flat starred in the movie *The Last Jedi* as the planet Crait.

SOUTH AMERICA

ATACAMA DESERT

The Atacama Desert is one of the driest places on Earth.

The desert sits on a 1,600 km long plateau (a fairly level area of ground quite high up) between the Andes mountains and the Pacific Ocean.

The Atacama is one of the oldest deserts in the world – some parts of it have had desert conditions for 200 million years.

It is the driest warm desert on the planet.

Some weather stations in the Atacama have never recorded rain.

In some areas of the desert, fog rolls in from the ocean bringing enough moisture for plants and animals to live.

Hummingbirds sometimes visit the desert to feed on insects.

The Atacama toad is a hardy creature that manages to live at the edges of the desert.

The super-clear air makes it one of the best places in the world to observe the night sky.

The desert is so dry and hostile that NASA has used it to test instruments for missions to Mars – which has a similarly hostile environment

Hostile conditions

SOUTH AMERICA

Hummingbird

Clear night sky

31

IGUAÇU NATIONAL PARK

The Iguaçu Falls, in Iguaçu National Park, stretch for 2.7 km, making them the largest waterfalls in the world.

WOW!

Iguaçu Falls lie on the border between Brazil and Argentina.

In the local languages, Guarani and Tupi, the name Iguaçu means 'big water'.

Islands on the edge divide the falls into many separate powerful waterfalls.

The park around the falls is home to the jaguar, the largest cat in the Americas.

The Iguaçu river has many yacare caiman, a member of the crocodile family.

The forests are rich in unusual birdlife, including the harpy eagle, toucan and parakeet.

Birds known as great dusky swifts even make their nests behind the falls, and can be seen flying through the falls themselves!

Rare creatures that live here include the giant otter and the giant anteater.

The area has been inhabited by humans for over 10,000 years. Europeans first saw the falls in 1542.

Toucan

SOUTH AMERICA

Giant otter

Giant anteater

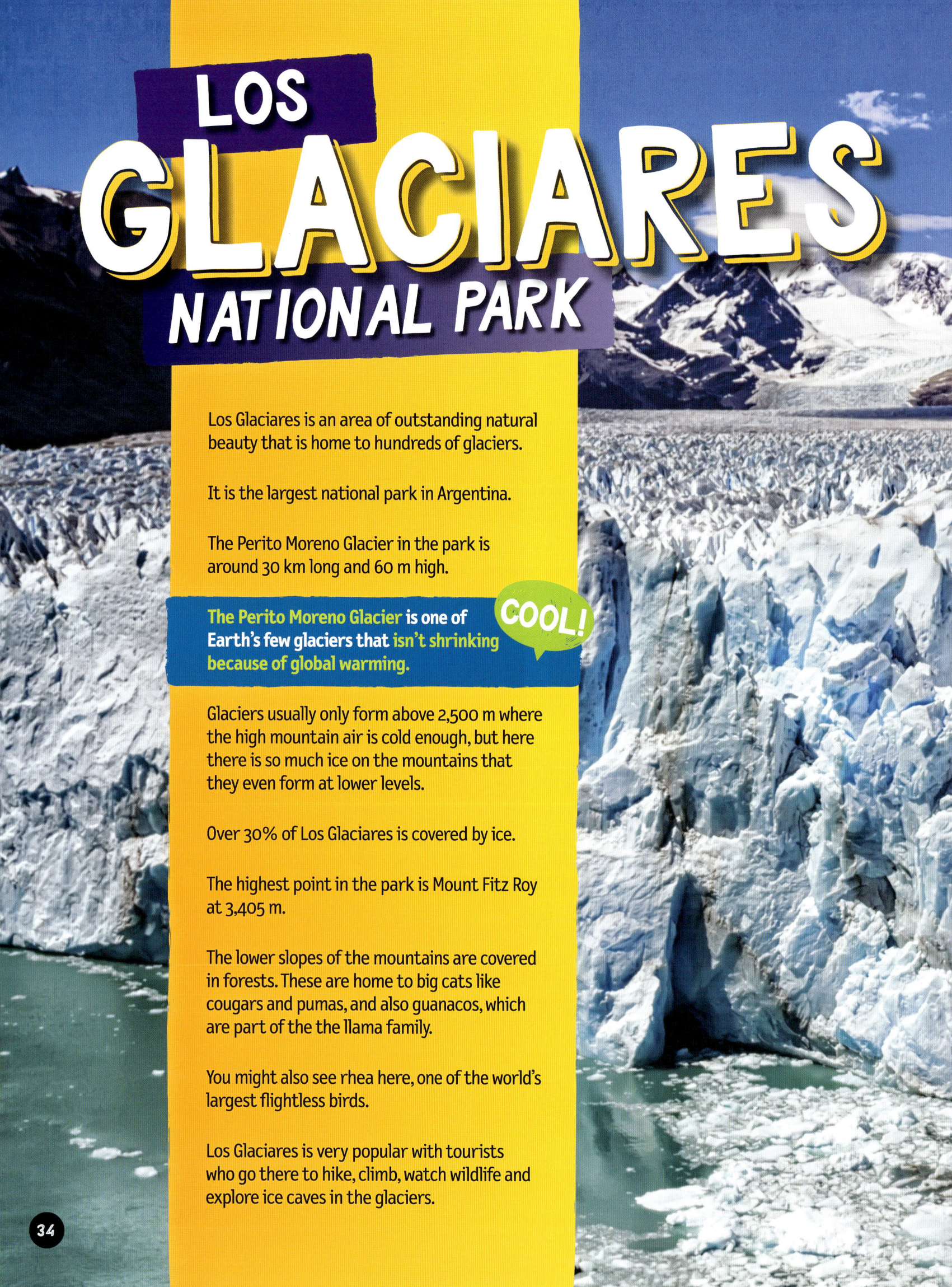

LOS GLACIARES NATIONAL PARK

Los Glaciares is an area of outstanding natural beauty that is home to hundreds of glaciers.

It is the largest national park in Argentina.

The Perito Moreno Glacier in the park is around 30 km long and 60 m high.

The Perito Moreno Glacier is one of Earth's few glaciers that isn't shrinking because of global warming. COOL!

Glaciers usually only form above 2,500 m where the high mountain air is cold enough, but here there is so much ice on the mountains that they even form at lower levels.

Over 30% of Los Glaciares is covered by ice.

The highest point in the park is Mount Fitz Roy at 3,405 m.

The lower slopes of the mountains are covered in forests. These are home to big cats like cougars and pumas, and also guanacos, which are part of the the llama family.

You might also see rhea here, one of the world's largest flightless birds.

Los Glaciares is very popular with tourists who go there to hike, climb, watch wildlife and explore ice caves in the glaciers.

SOUTH AMERICA

ANGEL FALLS

Angel Falls is the world's tallest waterfall.

The waterfall plummets 979 metres in a rainforest in Venezuela.

The falls are located in Canaima National Park, which is the second largest national park in Venezuela.

Canaima National Park is only accessible by air.

The fall is so long and so steep that the water can be completely turned to mist on the way down.

WOW!

If you dropped a stone from the top of the falls, it would take 14 seconds to hit the ground.

The waterfall flows over the edge of a tepui, or table-top mountain — 'tepui' means 'house of gods' in the local native tongue (Pemon). In Pemon, the falls are known as 'Kerepakupai-merú', — 'waterfall of the deepest place'.

The first outsider to discover the falls was an American pilot called Jimmie Angel — the falls are named after him.

Jimmie Angel first flew over the falls in 1933 when he was looking for minerals. Later, in 1937, he landed his plane near the top of the waterfall but it got stuck in the mud, and it took him 11 days to walk back to civilisation.

Angel Falls and the surrounding Canaima National Park are home to more than 550 species of birds and 500 species of orchids, as well as stunningly-marked ocelots and pumas.

Macaw

SOUTH AMERICA

Orchid

Ocelot

LENÇÓIS MARANHENSES
NATIONAL PARK

Lençóis Maranhenses is a vast area of sapphire-blue pools set in bright white 'hills' of sand, known as dunes.

The dunes were named after the Portuguese word for 'bedsheets' because of their spectacular white sand. COOL!

Each pool (also known as a lagoon) is around 100 m long and 3 m deep.

The pools are freshwater — filled by rain that falls between January and June.

In the dry season the pools evaporate completely.

The lagoons are part of a national park that stretches along 70 km of Brazil's Atlantic coast, and reaches 50 km inland.

Many of the lagoons are home to fish and insects, including the unusual-looking wolf-fish.

The dunes are created by strong winds. They blow sand brought downstream by rivers back inland.

The protected area around the dunes is a safe habitat for several endangered animals.

Endangered species that live in the area include the scarlet ibis, the neotropical otter, the oncilla and the West Indian manatee.

Scarlet ibis

SOUTH AMERICA

Neotropical otter

Oncilla

CAÑO CRISTALES

Caño Cristales is better known as the **'River of Five Colours'** or the **'Liquid Rainbow'**, thanks to its stunning colours.

COOL!

The river bed looks multicoloured – yellow, green, blue, black and bright red.

This fantastic colour show only happens for a brief period between the wet season and the dry season.

The river flows over quartzite rocks that were formed over a billion years ago.

It winds through an area in Colombia where the Amazon rainforest, a drier savannah plain (large grassy plain) and the Andes mountains all come together.

The mix of ecosystems in the area creates unique flora and fauna.

There are more than 2,000 species of plants, 550 species of birds, 100 reptiles and 1,200 insects in the region around the river, but there aren't any fish in Caño Cristales itself!

Endangered creatures that live here include anteaters, jaguars, cougars and eight species of monkey.

The area is far away from towns and communities, and visitors have to fly in specially to see the river.

You can swim in the river but you are not allowed to wear sunscreen in case it damages the fragile ecosystem.

SOUTH AMERICA

GALÁPAGOS
ISLANDS

The Galápagos Islands are such an amazing place that 97% of the area is protected as a national park.

The Galápagos Islands, off the coast of Ecuador, form one of the most volcanically active areas in the world. They have 13 active volcanoes.

The scientist Charles Darwin studied birds on the islands and formed ideas about how life changes, or evolves, over a long period of time.

The islands are named after the giant tortoises that live there. Galápagos is Spanish for tortoise.

Galápagos giant tortoises can weigh over 400 kg and live to be 170. They can survive up to one year without food or water!

The islands have the only species of penguin found north of the equator.

There is no light pollution here, making the night skies some of the most dazzling on the planet.

Marine iguanas are the world's only seagoing lizards. They live here and nowhere else.

The islands have the same length of day and night all year round — 12 hours of each. This is because they straddle the equator.

The blue-footed booby — famous for its brightly coloured feet — is a common seabird here.

Giant tortoise

SOUTH AMERICA

Marine iguana

Blue-footed booby

FERNANDO DE NORONHA
& ATOL DAS ROCAS

Fernando de Noronha and Atol das Rocas are groups of islands that form part of the Brazilian Atlantic Islands. You can find everything from tropical beaches to mountains, jungles and mangroves here!

Fernando de Noronha is a group of 21 islands and smaller islets.

The islands here are the visible parts of a range of submerged mountains that were created by volcanoes. COOL!

The biggest island is 10 km long and 3.5 km wide, but the bottom of this huge volcanic mass lies 756 m under the surface of the sea.

Dolphin Bay is famous for its spinner dolphins, which often do cool acrobatics in the surf!

Humpback whales, pilot whales and melon-headed whales swim in the waters around the islands.

The seas here are an important breeding ground for tuna, sharks and two species of turtles.

Reefs and shallow lagoons have created a natural aquarium for scuba divers to enjoy.

The islands have two special lizards that are found only here: the Noronha worm lizard and the Noronha skink.

Atol das Rocas is the only atoll (ring-shaped coral reef) in the South Atlantic Ocean.

Spinner dolphin

SOUTH AMERICA

Yellowfin tuna

Noronha skink

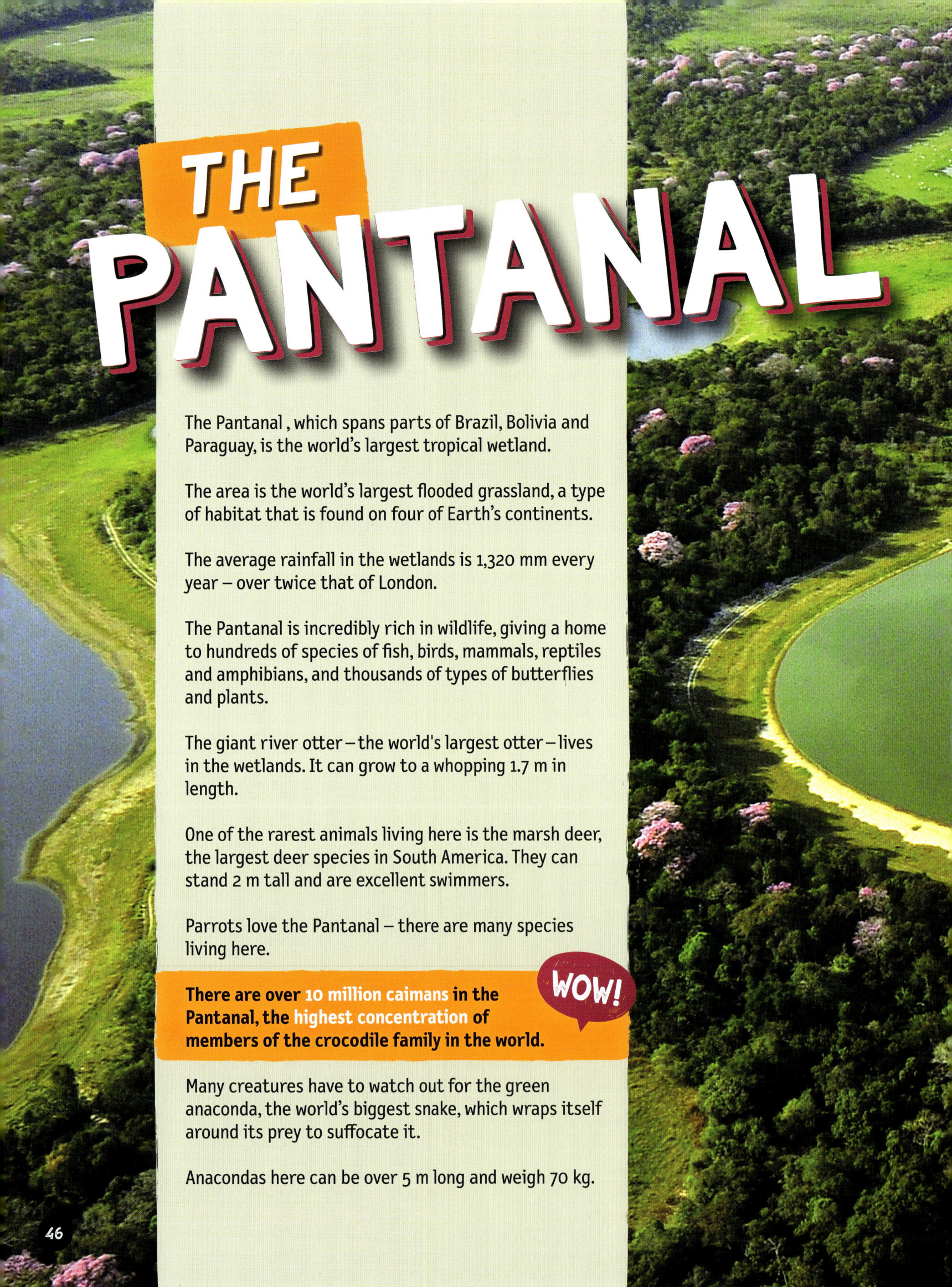

THE PANTANAL

The Pantanal, which spans parts of Brazil, Bolivia and Paraguay, is the world's largest tropical wetland.

The area is the world's largest flooded grassland, a type of habitat that is found on four of Earth's continents.

The average rainfall in the wetlands is 1,320 mm every year – over twice that of London.

The Pantanal is incredibly rich in wildlife, giving a home to hundreds of species of fish, birds, mammals, reptiles and amphibians, and thousands of types of butterflies and plants.

The giant river otter – the world's largest otter – lives in the wetlands. It can grow to a whopping 1.7 m in length.

One of the rarest animals living here is the marsh deer, the largest deer species in South America. They can stand 2 m tall and are excellent swimmers.

Parrots love the Pantanal – there are many species living here.

There are over 10 million caimans in the Pantanal, the highest concentration of members of the crocodile family in the world. WOW!

Many creatures have to watch out for the green anaconda, the world's biggest snake, which wraps itself around its prey to suffocate it.

Anacondas here can be over 5 m long and weigh 70 kg.

SOUTH AMERICA

THE AMAZON RIVER

The Amazon River travels for 6,500 km across South America to reach its destination in the South Atlantic Ocean.

More water flows in the Amazon than in the next seven largest world rivers combined! WOW!

Although the Amazon is the world's largest river, the Nile is slightly longer at 6,650 km.

At the mouth of the Amazon river, there is an island – Isla Marajó – that is the size of Switzerland!

The Amazon is home to some strange creatures: mata mata turtles and huge anacondas to name a few.

It's also home to the fierce arapaima, one of the world's biggest freshwater fish that not only has teeth on the roof of its mouth, but also on its tongue!

In the dry season the Amazon can be 9 km wide, but in the wet season it can be 48 km wide!

Before the Amazon reaches the sea, it flows through many South American countries including Brazil, Peru and Colombia.

The Amazon has a tidal bore, the Pororoca, that can send waves 4 m high up to 800 km inland.

In 2007, Martin Strel swam the whole length of the Amazon River. It took him 66 days!

Mata mata turtle

SOUTH AMERICA

Anaconda

Arapaima

HUASCARÁN NATIONAL PARK

With snow-crowned peaks, emerald lakes and unique wildlife, Huascarán National Park is a jewel of the natural world.

The park is in Peru and includes the peaks of Cordillera Blanca – the world's highest tropical mountain range.

At 6,768 m, Huascarán is the highest mountain in Peru.

With high mountains near the equator, the park has a variety of environments, from grasslands to rugged snowy mountains.

The area is a haven for the Queen of the Andes, the largest plant in the pineapple family.

The Queen of the Andes has similar features to a pineapple and grows to 15 m high. It can produce 20,000 flowers over three months.

The park features the largest area of glaciers in the tropics, with 660 glaciers and 300 glacial lakes.

Wild cats living here include the colocolo, the Andean mountain cat and the puma.

WOW!

The **spectacled bear** here is the **only** bear to originally come from **South America**. It has dark fur with light brown face markings that can look like **goggles**.

Andean condors soar silently above the valleys. They are one of the world's largest birds, with a huge wingspan.

Queen of the Andes

SOUTH AMERICA

Colocolo

Spectacled bear

MANU
NATIONAL PARK

Manu is a vast national park that covers an area between the Andes Mountains and the Amazon River basin.

The protected area is largely untouched by humans. It is almost the size of Wales but doesn't have a single road.

There are tribes of native people in the park who have never made any contact with the outside world. *WOW!*

At the heart of the park is the Manu river. This starts life as whitewater streams in the mountains, then winds its way through lowland forests, before joining the mighty Madre de Dios River and later the Amazon.

Among the 200 mammal species are the giant otter, giant armadillo and 13 different species of primates.

The largest rodent in the world, the capybara, lives in the park.

The capybara is related to guinea pigs, but it can grow much bigger — to over 1.3 m long, and can weigh over 70 kg.

There are eight species of felines in the forest, including the jaguar, puma, and the elusive and endangered Andean mountain cat.

The incredible variety of life here has astonished scientists and given them new knowledge of tropical forests.

An incredible 850 species of birds, like the swallow tanager, have been spotted in the park.

Capybara

SOUTH AMERICA

Jaguar

Swallow tanager

53

NORTH AMERICA

Kluane, Wrangell-St Elias and Glacier Bay

1 Cave of Crystals
2 Great Blue Hole
3 Talamanca Range – La Amistad Reserve
4 Death Valley
5 Hawaii Volcanoes National Park
6 Barringer Crater
7 Gros Morne National Park
8 Everglades National Park
9 Yellowstone National Park
10 Grand Canyon National Park
11 Great Smoky Mountains National Park
12 Kluane, Wrangell–St Elias and Glacier Bay
13 Ilulissat Icefjord
14 Dinosaur Provincial Park
15 Yosemite National Park
16 Monarch Butterfly Biosphere Reserve
17 Islands of the Gulf of California
18 Nahanni National Park
19 Carlsbad Caverns National Park
20 The Pitons

Ilulissat Icefjord

Yellowstone National Park

Talamanca Range – La Amistad Reserve

CAVE OF CRYSTALS

The Cave of Crystals is an underground cavern in Mexico that contains gigantic crystals of the mineral gypsum.

Some of the largest crystals are 1.2 m in diameter and 11 m long.

Gypsum has many uses, including fertiliser and plaster.

Gypsum is even used to make blackboard chalk!

The Cave of Crystals lies 300 m under the Earth's surface.

Inside the cave is very hot, with an air temperature of 58°C and over 90% humidity.

The cave is so hot and humid that any visit longer than 10 minutes could be deadly!

The crystals grow very slowly, so the largest ones have taken around 1 million years to form.

Scientists have found dormant microbes (microbes that have slowed right down) in the crystals that could be 50,000 years old.

The cave is part of a mine that also produces lead, zinc and silver.

NORTH AMERICA

GREAT BLUE HOLE

The Great Blue Hole is a perfectly round sinkhole in a coral reef off the coast of Belize.

Sinkholes are formed when the roof of a hollowed-out cavern collapses.

The hole began to form 150,000 years ago when sea levels were much lower.

It was originally a limestone cavern that was eroded by rain and flowing fresh water.

As the sea level rose after the last Ice Age, the cavern was flooded.

The hole is 318 m across and 124 m deep.

You could fit three football pitches across the width of the hole. WOW!

Parrotfish, reef sharks and hammerhead sharks can often be seen in the hole.

The hole was made famous by the French diver and explorer Jacques Cousteau.

Today, scuba divers visit to enjoy the hole's crystal-clear water. Only experienced divers, however, are allowed to dive there as it's thought to be a deep and complex dive.

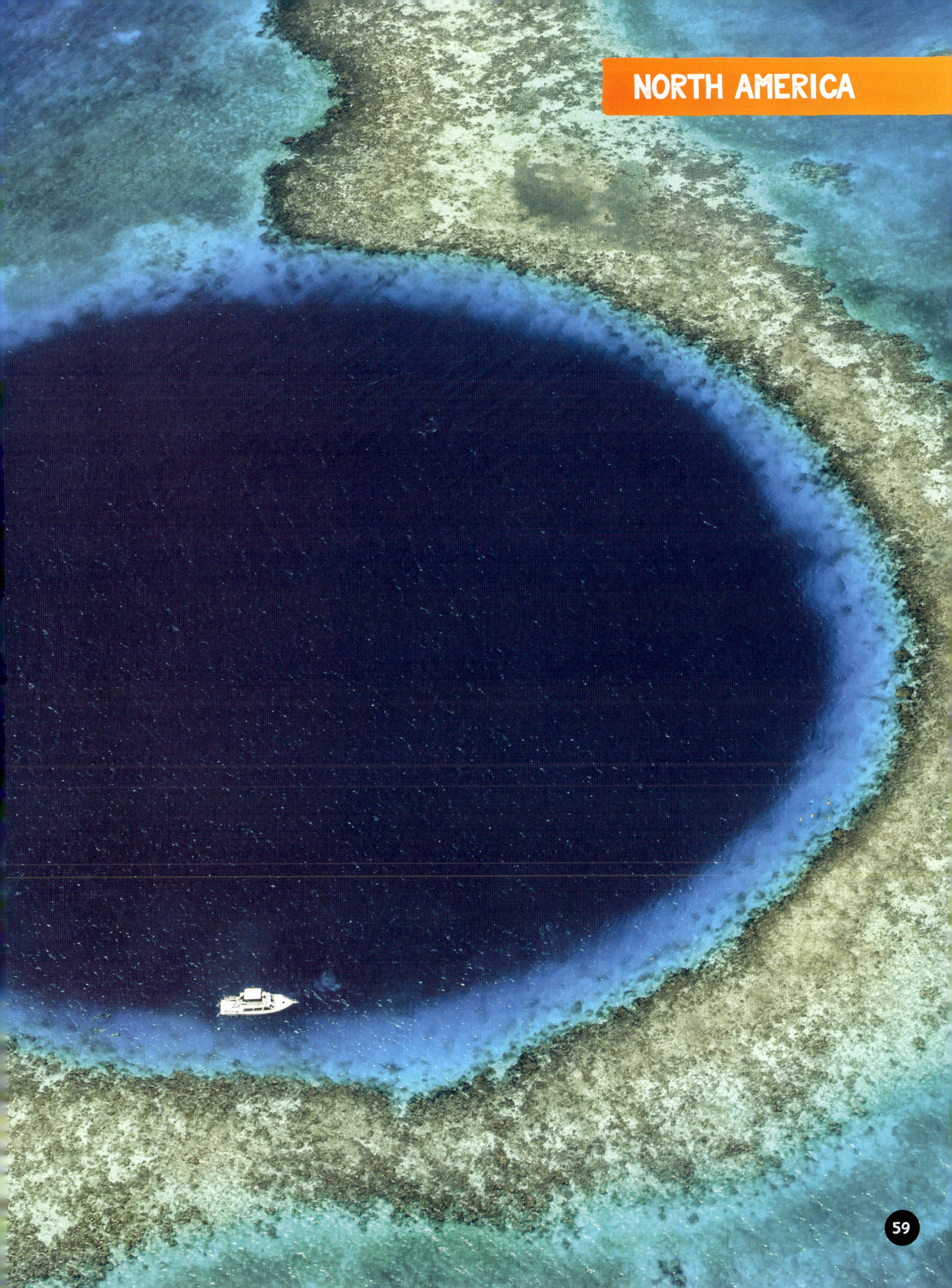

NORTH AMERICA

TALAMANCA RANGE – LA AMISTAD RESERVE

The rugged Talamanca range has some exceptionally beautiful mountain landscapes.

The range is one of the biggest natural areas of wild forest in central America, extending along the border between Panama and Costa Rica.

The range lies on the isthmus, or narrow strip of land, that lies between North and South America.

The land bridge that the range lies on formed about 3 million years ago, which is quite recent in geological time.

Because of its location between the two continents, the range shares plants and animals with both North and South America.

The peaks of the mountains act as 'sky islands' for many species of plants and animals, giving them a safe home, away from certain predators. WOW!

There are five species of big cats roaming the park: pumas, ocelots, margay, jaguars and jaguarundis.

The forests have over 600 species of birds, including the striking quetzal, bare-necked umbrellabird and the Talamanca hummingbird.

In 2006, researchers discovered 12 plant species, 1 dung beetle species, 15 amphibian and 3 reptile species that were completely new to science.

The ornate spider monkey, Central American tapir and black-crowned squirrel monkey are some of the endangered species that call this range home.

Hummingbird

NORTH AMERICA

Ornate spider monkey

Margay

DEATH VALLEY

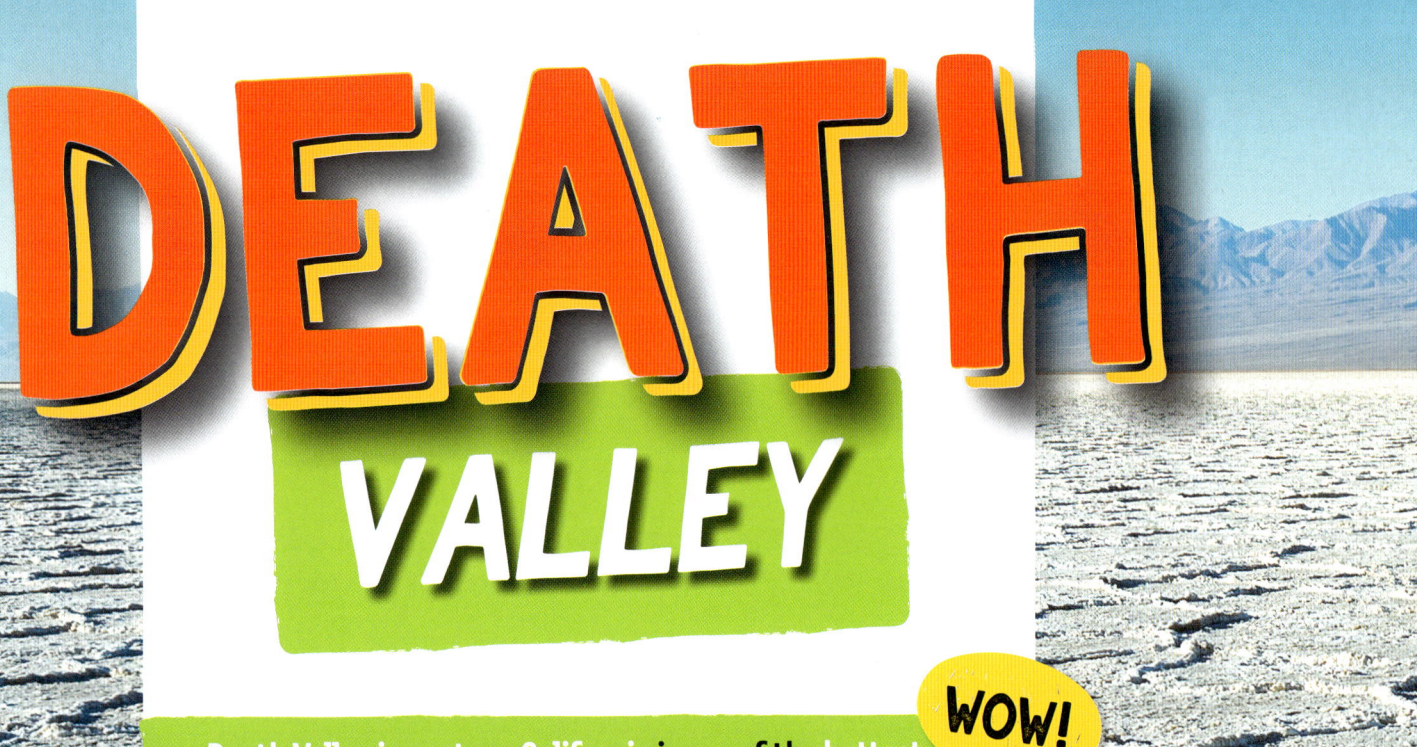

Death Valley in eastern California is one of the hottest places on Earth, regularly reaching more than 50°C.

WOW!

At 86 m below sea level, it is the lowest place in North America.

Despite its name, Death Valley can burst with life when downpours cause wildflowers to bloom.

Sometimes it seems like rocks move across the desert on their own — this is thanks to strong winds and ice.

Some of the rarest fish in the world live here — Devils Hole Pupfish can survive in pools that reach 34 °C.

The roadrunner, which featured in a cartoon with Wile E. Coyote and is a bird related to the cuckoo, is one of the most common creatures living here.

Death Valley was given its name by gold prospectors. People on the hunt for gold had to cross Death Valley to get to the gold fields. Many didn't make it to the other side because of the valley's extreme conditions.

The white areas in the valley (like in the picture) are salt flats left behind by evaporated lakes.

Sometimes it doesn't rain in Death Valley for more than a year!

Sand dunes in Death Valley can be over 200 m high — that's taller than St Paul's Cathedral in London.

NORTH AMERICA

HAWAII VOLCANOES NATIONAL PARK

Hawaii Volcanoes National Park includes two of the world's most active volcanoes – Kīlauea and Mauna Loa.

You can look inside Kīlauea thanks to several webcams set up around the crater.

If you catch a volcano erupting, it can look like a firework display as lava pours into the ocean.

Mauna Loa is the largest active volcano on Earth. It has been erupting for at least 700,000 years.

COOL!

Hawaii is the most remote group of islands with a sizeable population on Earth. The islands lie over 3,000 km from the nearest mainland.

As well as its amazing volcanoes, the park is one of the most fascinating wildlife landscapes in the world.

Over 90% of Hawaii's plants and animals are found only in the Hawaiian islands.

The only land mammal native to Hawaii is the Hawaiian hoary bat. It is endangered.

Hawaii has some unique caterpillars – they are the only ones in the world that are carnivorous (meat-eaters)! Eupithecia, or the Hawaiian carnivorous caterpillar, loves to feast on insects.

One of the world's largest dragonflies lives in the forests here. The giant Hawaiian darner has a wingspan of up to 15 cm.

Kilauea volcano

NORTH AMERICA

Hawaiian waterfall

Hawaiian hoary bat

BARRINGER CRATER

The Barringer Crater in Arizona is one of the best-preserved meteorite craters on Earth.

The crater was formed 50,000 years ago when a lump of iron and nickel from space smashed into the Earth's surface.

The meteorite was 50 m across and was travelling at around 50,000 km/h. WOW!

The crater is 1,200 m in diameter, meaning you could fit 24 Olympic-size swimming pools end-to-end across it!

It is 170 m deep and has a rim that stands 45 m above the surrounding plain.

Over time the crater has been eroded. Originally it was 30 m deeper and its rim was 20 m higher.

The impact of the meteorite had the explosive power of millions of tonnes of TNT — a powerful explosive.

In the 1960s and 1970s, astronauts trained in the crater for the Apollo missions to the Moon.

This is not the largest meteor crater on Earth. At 300 km across, Vredefort crater in South Africa is around 250 times bigger.

There is a visitor centre on the north rim of the the crater that includes a movie theatre, gift shop and observation areas where you can peer inside the crater.

NORTH AMERICA

GROS MORNE NATIONAL PARK

Gros Morne in Canada's Newfoundland and Labrador province has a freshwater fjord (inlet) with towering cliffs, the highest waterfall in eastern North America, sandy beaches, sea stacks and caves, not to mention lots of impressive wildlife.

In the last Ice Age, glaciers carved the land creating fjords, an alpine plateau and waterfalls.

Western Brook Pond is a 30-km long fjord that was carved out by glaciers thousands of years ago.

The fjord does not connect to the sea, but is filled with extremely pure fresh water.

The park is a geological treasure house where huge tectonic plates have crashed into each other and shaped the crust of the Earth.

COOL!

Common wild animals in the park include Arctic foxes, caribou, black bears, snowshoe hares, red squirrels, lynxes, river otters and beavers.

The mountains in the park are the remains of a larger range that formed 1.2 billion years ago.

The park has a barren area called the Tablelands. The rocks are toxic and nothing can survive here.

There are lots of moose in the park, and each one needs to eat around 32 kg of plants every day.

The bays and coves around the coast are visited by seals, humpback whales, orcas, dolphins and harbour porpoises.

Arctic fox

NORTH AMERICA

Tablelands

Moose

EVERGLADES
NATIONAL PARK

The Everglades in Florida are the largest subtropical wilderness in the United States.

The area is a network of waterways, coastal mangroves, marshes and pinewoods.

Everglades National Park was the first national park created to protect a fragile ecosystem—an area where plants and animals depend on each other to survive.

The whole Everglades area covers 20,202 km², which is almost the size of Wales! COOL!

Hundreds of species of animals live here, including many endangered ones.

The area is home to the very shy Florida panther. There are fewer than 250 of these large cats left in the wild.

The park is an important breeding ground for waterbirds, including spoonbills, pelicans and herons.

Alligators, crocodiles and manatees thrive here.

It's the only place in the world where American alligators and crocodiles live in the wild together. Normally crocodiles live in salt water and alligators prefer fresh water, but here, they all live in the same environment.

Humans introduced Burmese pythons into the Everglades, and they became an invasive species. A programme was set up to remove these snakes as they were preying on important animals like deer and alligators, causing their numbers to drop dramatically.

Rosette spoonbill

NORTH AMERICA

Pelican

Alligator

YELLOWSTONE
NATIONAL PARK

Yellowstone National Park, spanning parts of the states of Wyoming, Montana and Idaho, was created in 1872, making it the world's first official national park.

Yellowstone's mountains, lakes, canyons and rivers are home to hundreds of species of mammals, birds, fish, reptiles and amphibians.

The park lies over a large dormant supervolcano (a huge volcano that could cause serious damage if it erupted).

The volcano last erupted 630,000 years ago but it still powers the park's hot springs and geysers.

Many hot springs are brightly coloured (like the rainbow-coloured Grand Prismatic Pool, pictured on the right) thanks to **microbes** living in the mineral-rich water. **WOW!**

Half the world's active geysers lie inside the park.

A geyser is a large spurt of hot water and steam. The water is heated underground by magma (the incredibly hot material deep beneath the Earth's surface).

The geyser 'Old Faithful' erupts on average every 90 minutes to a height of more than 50 m.

Around 700 grizzly bears live in Yellowstone, as well as many black bears.

The park is a safe place for American bison, which were nearly hunted to extinction. When travelling on the roads around the park, drivers often find themselves in bison traffic jams!

Grizzly bear

NORTH AMERICA

Old Faithful erupting

Bison

GRAND CANYON NATIONAL PARK

The Grand Canyon is a spectacular steep-sided gorge in Arizona. It is sometimes called one of the seven natural wonders of the world.

The Grand Canyon is over 400 km long.

Some parts of the canyon are incredibly narrow, but at its widest it is 29 km across!

The canyon is 1,850 m deep in places — deep enough to stack six Eiffel Towers on top of each other.

COOL!

The canyon was cut into the landscape by the Colorado River.

The layers of rock in the canyon walls are colourful. They date back 2 billion years in places.

Scientists have found fossilised animal footprints that are 313 million years old in the canyon.

Coyotes and mountain lions are an important part of the canyon ecosystem.

Falcons, owls, hawks and condors can be seen soaring around the gorge.

Rock squirrels live in the park, and despite there being much bigger animals there, it is the rock squirrel that is the most dangerous to tourists. Every year the squirrels bite visitors who try to feed them!

Coyote

NORTH AMERICA

Californian condor

Horse Shoe Bend

GREAT SMOKY MOUNTAINS NATIONAL PARK

The Great Smoky Mountains National Park contains forests full of plants and animals, as well as the highest mountains in eastern North America.

It is the most-visited national park in the United States, with 12 million visitors a year. WOW!

A whopping 95% of the park is forest.

There are more than 100 species of trees in the park.

The dense forests and lots of rain mean that over 19,000 types of plants and animals live here.

At least 200 species of birds and 50 species of fish thrive in the park.

Mammals include the black bear, raccoon, bobcat, coyote, skunk and chipmunk.

Lungless salamanders are unique amphibians found here – they 'breathe' through their skin!

Elk, the largest species of deer, were reintroduced to the park in 2001.

In late May to mid-June, synchronous fireflies light up the area with their synchronised flashing light patterns. They're actually beetles (not flies!) who flash their lights to attract a mate!

Black bear

NORTH AMERICA

Raccoon

Skunk

KLUANE, WRANGELL –ST ELIAS AND GLACIER BAY

Marmot

Kluane, Wrangell–St Elias and Glacier Bay park in Canada is home to spectacular glaciers and icefields.

The area of the park is 98,000 km² – that's bigger than Portugal. WOW!

The world's largest icefield that is not at the North or South poles lies inside the park.

Margerie Glacier is one of many huge glaciers here. It is 34 km long, 1.6 km wide and 110 m thick where it meets the sea.

Animals have to have thick coats to live here — the snowshoe hare, marmot and wolverine are all well-adapted to living in this chilly environment.

Predators in the park include the grizzly bear, Yukon wolf, coyote and lynx.

Sea lions and humpback whales swim in the coastal waters around the park — they also need a layer of blubber, or fat, to keep them warm.

The park is a haven for 120 species of birds, including golden and bald eagles.

The area is home to Mount Logan, the highest mountain in Canada measuring 5,959 m.

The park's incredible glaciers and landscapes earned it UNESCO World Heritage status in 1994.

NORTH AMERICA

Margerie Glacier

Bald eagle

ILULISSAT ICEFJORD

Ilulissat Icefjord on the west coast of Greenland is a steep-sided, 40 km-long valley carved by a glacier.

The icefjord is where the huge Jakobshavn Glacier meets the sea. Icebergs break off the glacier into the sea here.

Ilulissat takes its name from the Kalaallisut word for icebergs.

The Jakobshavn Glacier produces **more icebergs** than any other glacier in the **Northern Hemisphere**.

WOW!

Every year 35 billion tonnes of icebergs break off and float out of the fjord.

Some icebergs that form are very big — up to 1 km in height.

Large icebergs often get stuck on the sea bottom in the icefjord. It can take years for them to be smashed up by the glacier and the sea, and to float free.

Scientists have studied the Jakobshavn Glacier for over 250 years in order to help them understand climate change. Glaciers are melting as a result of global warming and scientists want to know why, and how we can prevent it.

The glacier is very fast moving. It moves forward 40 metres every day.

The waters around here are often visited by humpback, minke, fin and bowhead whales.

NORTH AMERICA

DINOSAUR PROVINCIAL PARK

Dinosaur remains

Dinosaur Provincial Park in Alberta, Canada is one of the best areas for dinosaur fossils in the world.

Approximately 35 dinosaur species have been discovered here. WOW!

The fossils and remains are found in rocks that were laid down around 75 million years ago.

Wind and water have eroded the rocks to reveal the fossils.

Fossils of 500 species of life have been found here.

The park's ecosystem includes prairies, badlands and riverside woods.

Badlands are dry areas with strange rocks and cliffs which are formed by erosion.

Rattlesnakes, bull snakes and garter snakes live in the park. Rattlesnakes rattle the end of their tail in order to warn predators to leave them alone!

Visitors to the park can join in with digs and look for fossils themselves!

You can even see fossilised dinosaur dung here – it's known as coprolite.

NORTH AMERICA

Rattlesnake

Coprolite

YOSEMITE
NATIONAL PARK

Yosemite National park in California is world famous for its granite cliffs, waterfalls, glaciers, meadows and rich wildlife.

El Capitan is a sheer rock face that rises 914 m from the valley floor of the park.

The granite rock that forms El Capitan glows bright red in the evening when it reflects the light of sunset.

The spectacular waterfall, Bridalveil Fall, is 188 m high.

The Yosemite landscape was carved by glaciers during the last Ice Age. There are still some glaciers in the park today.

In winter and spring, 'frazil ice' can flow in the park's creeks instead of water. This is when mist from the big waterfalls freezes into small crystals in mid-air. They join the flow of water in the stream below and make it look like the stream is full of slush! COOL!

Many giant sequoia grow here. They are the largest trees in the world, reaching 95 m high and 8 m in diameter.

Peregrine falcons – the world's fastest bird and animal – soar over the trees.

There are around 400 black bears living in the park, along with deer, coyote, cougars, marmots and bobcats.

The extremely rare Sierra Nevada red fox also lives in the park. It was spotted, on a webcam, in 2014 – the first sighting in 100 years!

El Capitan

NORTH AMERICA

Giant sequoia

Peregrine falcon

MONARCH BUTTERFLY
BIOSPHERE RESERVE

Every autumn a billion butterflies from North America return to the forest here in Mexico for the winter.

There are so many butterflies that they colour the trees orange and bend branches under their weight! WOW!

When the butterflies all take flight at the same time, their beating wings make the sound of light rain!

In spring, the butterflies set off on an 8-month migration — a very long journey — all the way to eastern Canada and back.

On the migration, four successive generations of butterflies are born and die. How they find their way back to the place they stay over winter is a mystery.

At least 70% of all the eastern monarch butterflies will come to the biosphere.

Monarchs migrate thousands of kilometres every year but fly at just 9 km/h, which is slower than average human jogging speed.

Monarchs can have a wingspan of more than 10 cm.

The butterflies particularly like oyumel fir trees, which only grow at high altitudes between 2,400 and 3,600 m.

Monarchs protect themselves from cold and storms by clustering closely together under the forest canopy.

NORTH AMERICA

ISLANDS
OF THE GULF OF CALIFORNIA

Manta ray

The Gulf of California is one of the most diverse seas on Earth for life. It has been nicknamed 'the Aquarium of the World'.

The Gulf of California is also known as the Sea of Cortés.

The gulf is long, thin and deep. It is 1,126 km long, 48–241 km wide and has an average depth of 818 m.

There are 37 large islands in the gulf and over 900 smaller islets. The two largest islands are Isla Ángel de la Guarda and Isla Tiburón.

The islands are very important nesting sites for thousands of seabirds.

Of the 891 fish species here, 90 of them live nowhere else.

Rare marine species in these waters include the manta ray, Humboldt squid and leatherback sea turtle.

39% of the world's sea-going mammal species and 33% of the world's cetacean species (water mammals including whales, dolphins and porpoises) live here.

Large cetaceans that can be seen here include the humpback whale, California gray whale, killer whale, fin whale, sperm whale and the **world's biggest animal**, the blue whale.

WOW!

The endangered vaquita, a type of small porpoise, lives in the waters here. There are thought to be fewer than 20 of these creatures left.

NORTH AMERICA

Humboldt squid

Leatherback sea turtle

NAHANNI
NATIONAL PARK

The South Nahanni River crashes through the Mackenzie Mountains in Canada in an awe-inspiring series of whitewater falls.

The river has carved four huge canyons through the mountains – First, Second, Third and Fourth Canyon.

The river canyons are up to 1,000 m deep.

500 million years ago, the rocks were formed as sediment at the bottom of an inland sea.

Over time, Earth's continents pressed together thrusting the rocks upwards to form mountains.

Fossils of sea creatures can still be found high in the mountains.

Glaciers carved out valleys here during several Ice Ages in the last 2 million years.

Virginia Falls is a thundering 90 m whitewater cascade that's almost twice the height of Niagara Falls. WOW!

Whitewater is created when a river gets steeper and air is trapped in the tumbling water.

The constant mist created by Virginia Falls allows several rare orchid species to grow nearby.

NORTH AMERICA

CARLSBAD CAVERNS NATIONAL PARK

There are more than 120 caves in the Carlsbad Caverns National Park in New Mexico.

The caves are remarkable for their large size and their beautiful rock formations.

The largest cavern is the Big Room, which is 1,220 m long, 191 m wide, and 78 m high.

The Big Room is the largest cave chamber in the whole of North America.

250 million years ago, the area was the coastline of an inland sea where a reef was created by marine creatures.

The caverns formed when a limestone reef was lifted up and later eroded by water over millions of years.

The forces that formed these caves are **still at work**, allowing scientists to study them in action. WOW!

Lechuguilla Cave is a large cavern famous for its amazing cave structures, or speleothems.

Speleothems are structures in caves formed by water and minerals. They include stalactites and stalagmites, which are mineral deposits that grow from the ceiling downwards (stalactite) or ground upwards (stalagmite).

Lechuguilla Cave has 'chandeliers' made of gypsum that are more than 6 m long.

Stalactites in the caves

NORTH AMERICA

Cave entrance

Lechuguilla Cave

THE PITONS

The Pitons are a striking pair of volcanic peaks in Saint Lucia covered in thick forest.

The Pitons are volcanic plugs, formed when hot liquid lava rising from inside the Earth hardens inside a volcano.

COOL!

There are active fumaroles in the area — holes in the planet's crust that spew out steam and volcanic gases.

Gros Piton is 798 m high and Petit Piton is 743 m high. They rise straight up from the sea.

The Pitons are in a protected area that includes marine, jungle and mountain habitats.

Forests cover over 70% of the whole island of Saint Lucia.

Spectacular coral reefs cover almost 60% of the coastal waters surrounding the Pitons.

Hawksbill turtles visit coves on the island, and whale sharks and pilot whales swim in the seas.

The Pitons are a symbol of Saint Lucia and sailors have used them to help navigate the seas for centuries.

There are over 150 plant species on the Pitons, including 8 types of rare trees.

Hawksbill turtle

NORTH AMERICA

Whale shark

Pilot whale

AFRICA

1. Kilimanjaro National Park
2. Victoria Falls
3. Whale Valley
4. Serengeti National Park
5. Lake Natron
6. Deadvlei
7. Rainforests of the Atsinanana
8. W-arly-Pendjari Area
9. Aldabra Atoll
10. Bwindi Impenetrable Forest
11. Danakil Depression
12. Virunga National Park
13. Okavango Delta
14. Tsingy de Bemaraha
15. Vallée de Mai Nature Reserve

W-arly-Pendjari Area

KILIMANJARO
NATIONAL PARK

At 5,895 m, Mount Kilimanjaro in Tanzania is the highest mountain in Africa.

Mount Kilimanjaro is not part of a range—it is the highest single free-standing mountain in the world.

COOL!

Mount Kilimanjaro is a dormant volcano, meaning it *could* erupt again one day, but it last erupted about 200,000 years ago!

The top of Kilimanjaro has a permanent ice cap with glaciers.

The summit ice cap is shrinking. Between 1912 and 2011, Kilimanjaro lost 85% of its ice.

Most of the ice on Kilimanjaro will disappear by 2040.

It usually takes at least six days to trek to the summit of Mount Kilimanjaro, but professional athletes have managed it in around just seven hours!

The lower slopes of the mountain are covered in forest. Monkeys, bushbabies and leopards all live in the trees.

Elephants, warthogs, zebras and giraffes roam the plains and grasslands around the mountain.

One of the rarest creatures on the mountain is the tiny Kilimanjaro shrew.

Elephant

AFRICA

Warthog

Bushbaby

VICTORIA FALLS

Victoria Falls is one of the world's largest waterfalls.

The falls are on the Zambezi river and lie on the border between Zambia and Zimbabwe.

With a drop of 108 m, Victoria Falls is twice the height of North America's Niagara Falls.

The falls stretch for 1,708 m, creating the largest curtain of falling water in the world!

National parks around the falls are home to animals including elephants, Cape buffalo, giraffes, zebras, lions, leopards and cheetahs.

Raptors (birds of prey) such as the Taita falcon, black eagle, peregrine falcon and augur buzzard soar over the gorges below the falls, looking for food.

When the falls are in flood, it can be hard to see them due to the mist and flying spray they create.

During the day, rainbows form in the mist around the falls, and at night you can sometimes see a moonbow. COOL!

In the local Sotho language, the falls are called Mosi-oa-Tunya — which means 'The Smoke That Thunders'.

Water levels in the Zambezi river start to drop around September to December, meaning that brave swimmers can get right up to the edge of Victoria Falls and peer down into the chasm below!

Leopard

AFRICA

Moonbow

Black eagle

WHALE VALLEY

Whale Valley, or Wadi Al-Hitan, in Egypt is a desert site known for its fossils of early whales.

The fossils here show how whales evolved from land animals to sea-going creatures – they show that before whales became the creatures we know today, they went through a middle stage where they still kept their back legs!

The largest skeleton found at the site was 21 m long.

Some fossils are so well preserved that you can see the last meal the whales ate! WOW!

Fossilised creatures here lived 50 million years ago, when the desert was a shallow sea.

As well as whales, there are also fossils of ancient crocodiles, sharks, rays, turtles and sea snakes.

The fossils were first discovered in 1902, but they weren't properly studied until the 1980s.

It became a World Heritage Site in 2005.

Wild animals living near the valley include the North African jackal, Egyptian mongoose, African wildcat and fennec fox.

Sand dunes here are always moving and changing thanks to the wind.

Egyptian mongoose

AFRICA

Rocks in Whale Valley

Fennec fox

SERENGETI
NATIONAL PARK

Nile crocodile

The plains of the Serengeti National Park in Tanzania are filled with remarkable wildlife like the wildebeest, lion, zebra, leopard, cheetah, rhinoceros, giraffe and golden wolf.

Serengeti comes from the Maasai word 'siringit' meaning 'endless plains,' which refers to the huge 30,000 km^2 area covered by the park.

Every year the park's 1.5 million wildebeest go on the world's longest migration on land. They travel in search of fresh food and better water. WOW!

Wildebeest have to make a dangerous river crossing past 3,000 crocodiles. For every one wildebeest captured by the crocodiles, another 50 drown.

More than 500 types of birds and 300 types of mammals live in the park.

There are 3,000 lions in the park – more than in any other place in Africa.

Nile crocodiles are the largest freshwater predator in Africa and many live in the Serengeti National Park. They can be huge and reach 6 m in length.

Rhinos also live in the park but they are endangered. Sadly, only 31 remain here.

Cheetahs are the world's fastest land animal, and can run at 128 km/h when chasing their dinner!

Humans are forbidden to live in the park.

LAKE NATRON

Lake Natron in Tanzania has a very high amount of salts dissolved in it.

The lake is large — 57 km long by 22 km wide — but only 3 m deep.

The lake's shallowness causes a lot of its water to evaporate, leaving more and more salt behind.

The lake's saltiness and its very high temperature of up to 60 °C mean that only a few creatures can live here. WOW!

Algae that thrive on the salt live in the lake. They are responsible for turning the water red.

The lake is one of the few breeding grounds for flamingos — millions of them breed here every year!

If an animal falls into the water, the high salt levels in the water 'calcify' it, and make the animal look like it's been turned to stone.

The lake is very difficult to access and wasn't visited by explorers until 1954.

It lies in a rift valley, where two of Earth's tectonic plates are splitting apart.

Within 10 million years, the tectonic plates under the lake will completely split and a new ocean will form here.

Flamingo

AFRICA

Algae turn the water red

Calcified animal remains

DEADVLEI

Deadvlei is a dry white clay riverbed in Namibia dotted with eerie dead trees.

Deadvlei lies in the Namib-Naukluft Park which covers nearly 50,000 km² and is one of the largest game parks in Africa.

Deadvlei means 'dead marsh', which is what Deadvlei is!

Deadvlei was formed by a river which was later cut off. It then dried out, leaving the clay base which was turned white by the sun.

The intense sun has killed and scorched the thorn trees into black skeletons. It's so dry here that the dead trees can't even rot down! WOW!

A few small plants do, however, manage to live here by taking water from the morning mist.

The Namib fog beetle also survives here by collecting fog droplets on its wings.

The sand dunes surrounding the area are among the highest in the world — the highest is almost 400 m tall!

The dunes change colour over time — the older the dune, the brighter shade of orange it is.

Photographers love to come here to capture the contrast in colours — from the dry white clay riverbed to black dead trees, to the bright orange dunes.

AFRICA

RAINFORESTS OF THE ATSINANANA

The Rainforests of the Atsinanana on Madagascar have animals and plants that are found nowhere else on Earth.

These rainforests are on the east coast of Madagascar, where it is very rainy in the wet season (November to April).

90% of the island's wildlife is found only here.

Madagascar separated from all other land masses 60 million years ago, so its creatures evolved in their own unique way.

Madagascar is the fourth-largest island in the world — it's bigger than France. *WOW!*

The ring-tailed lemur is one of over 100 species of lemurs that only live in Madagascar.

There are 170 types of palm trees on Madagascar, three times as many as on the whole continent of Africa!

Over 170 bird species live in the rainforests, including the endangered Madagascar serpent eagle and red owl.

The incredibly shy aye-aye is a lemur with very long fingers. These help it find grubs hiding in trees.

The Malagasy giant rat can leap 1 metre in the air.

Ring-tailed lemur

AFRICA

Aye-aye

Madagascar serpent eagle

W-ARLY-PENDJARI AREA

W-Arly-Pendjari is a protected area made up of multiple large wildlife parks joined together.

The park land is spread across three countries: Niger, Benin and Burkina Faso.

The park has a huge range of different habitats, from forests and river wetlands to open savannah (large grassy plains) and steep sandstone hills.

There are many large mammals living here, including the elephant, lion, hippopotamus, African buffalo and antelope.

Hippos wallow in the rivers here. They can weigh a staggering **1,500 kg** and **run at 30 km/h**.

WOW!

The closest mammal relative to hippos are whales!

The park is famous for its rich bird life, with over 350 species living here.

The hooded vulture lives in the area but in very small numbers. It feeds mainly on dead animals, but also insects.

The very rare West African wild dog may also still live in some places in the park.

West African wild dogs are sociable creatures and live in packs with 10 to 40 members.

Hippo

ALDABRA ATOLL

The Aldabra Atoll in the Indian Ocean is the largest raised coral reef in the world.

A raised coral reef is one that is high enough above the sea to allow soil to develop, and plants and animals to live in it.

Aldabra is the world's second-largest coral atoll, or ring-shaped reef.

Aldabra has a shallow lagoon in the centre that is surrounded by 4 large islands and 40 smaller ones.

The atoll is 34 km long and 13 km wide.

The atoll is home to 100,000 giant tortoises, which can grow to over a metre long and weigh 250 kg.

COOL!

There are no sources of fresh water on the atoll, so giant tortoises living there get their water from their food.

An Aldabra giant tortoise called Adwaita was 250 years old when he died in 2006 — he was thought to be one of the world's oldest living animals, ever!

Aldabra is also home to nearly 300 species of plants.

The world's largest land crab, the coconut crab, lives here. They can be 1 m long and weigh up to 4.5 kg, and they can climb trees!

Mushroom raised coral

AFRICA

Giant tortoise

Coconut crab

BWINDI
IMPENETRABLE FOREST

WOW!

Half the world's population of the highly endangered **mountain gorillas** live in the jungles of Bwindi Impenetrable Forest in Uganda.

The forest has more than 1,000 flowering plant species, including 163 different types of trees.

It is protected as an animal sanctuary within a national park.

The park's standout creatures are the estimated 400 Bwindi gorillas that live high in the mountains.

Mountain gorillas live in groups of up to 30. All but one are female — the single male is known as a 'silverback'.

Temperatures high up in the mountains get cold, so mountain gorillas here have thicker, longer fur than other gorillas to keep them warm.

The forest is also a safe haven for colobus monkeys, chimpanzees, and many birds such as hornbills and turacos.

The whole park is mountainous, with 60% of the land higher than 2,000 metres.

One of the rarest mammals to survive here is the rarely-seen African golden cat.

In the local language, Runyakitara, Bwindi comes from a word meaning 'a place full of darkness'.

Gorillas

AFRICA

Colobus monkey

Turaco

DANAKIL DEPRESSION

Three of the Earth's tectonic plates tearing apart have created the Danakil Depression, a land of acid lakes and fuming volcanoes.

WOW!

This alien-looking landscape in Ethiopia is 125 m below sea level, making it one of the lowest places on the planet.

The Awash River flows through the area before completely drying up in a chain of salt lakes – it never reaches the sea.

Gaet'ale Pond lies over a hot spring in the Danakil Depression. It is the saltiest body of water on Earth!

Lake Afrera is a salt lake with its own island – Franchetti Island is the lowest-lying island in the world.

In 1974, a 3.2 million-year-old humanoid skeleton was found in the area. 'Lucy' changed our understanding of human evolution.

Erta Ale is one of only eight volcanoes with a lava lake. This is the longest lasting lava lake and has existed since 1906.

At the Dallol volcano, hot springs belch out acidic liquid. The liquid forms bright green acid ponds.

Scientists studying the area have to wear gas masks to cope with the toxic gases and vapour!

Incredibly, bacteria live near the pools! They have adapted to the acidity, high temperatures and high salinity all at once in order to survive.

AFRICA

VIRUNGA
NATIONAL PARK

Virunga National Park in the Democratic Republic of the Congo is the oldest protected national park in Africa. It was established in 1925.

Mount Stanley is the park's highest peak at 5,109 m.

The mountains and forest protect over 1,000 species of mammals, birds, reptiles and amphibians.

There are more bird species in Virunga than in the whole of the UK. The striking Madagascar bee-eater lives here and digs its nest in sand banks.

There are 109 reptile species here, more than any other protected area in Africa.

Virunga is the only place on Earth with three types of great apes – the mountain gorilla, eastern lowland gorilla, and eastern chimpanzee.

COOL!

Virunga's southern landscape is known for its tropical forests and active volcanoes.

Critically endangered mountain gorillas live on the sides of Mikeno (a dormant – or 'sleeping' – volcano).

The park has the world's only facility that cares for orphaned mountain gorillas.

The park is looked after by a team of 689 rangers.

Baby mountain gorilla

AFRICA

Madagascar bee-eater

Eastern chimpanzee

OKAVANGO DELTA

The Okavango Delta in Botswana is a huge network of rivers that do not flow into any sea or ocean.

A river delta is a wide area of land made from sand and soil dropped by slow-moving rivers.

Every year the rivers flood to create a shallow wetland that attracts thousands of animals.

The delta is very flat, with less than 2 m difference in height across its area of 15,000 km².

Mountain rain in January and February causes a surge in the Okavango River that flows 1,200 km in one month.

Floodwaters spread over the entire delta over 4 months (March–June).

Some of the largest African land mammals – such as lions, leopards, rhinos, elephants and Cape buffalo – visit the Delta.

Natural rafts of papyrus – a wetland plant – float across the lagoon, and crocodiles often use them as shelter.

More than 400 species of birds visit the delta, including Pel's fishing owl, one of the largest owls in the world.

The Okavango Delta is home to over 70 fish species, including the 1.4 m long African sharptooth catfish – an eel-like fish that can breathe air!  WOW!

Antelope crossing the delta

AFRICA

Rhinoceros

Pel's fishing owl

TSINGY DE BEMARAHA

A forest of needle-like rocks makes Tsingy de Bemaraha Strict Nature Reserve in northwest Madagascar a dangerous but beautiful place to explore!

The sharp, pointed rock shapes have been carved from limestone by water.

The canyons between the sheer spikes and pinnacles are called 'grikes'. These grikes can be over 100 m deep!

Many species that live here are found nowhere else on Earth, including a red rat and a miniscule chameleon.

Like blocks of flats, the rocky towers have different levels that give shelter to different creatures at each 'floor'.

Sifakas and other species of **lemurs** use the tsingy as a kind of **motorway**, **leaping** from **spire to spire** on their way to fruit trees. *COOL!*

Fruit bats, parrots and bees all use holes in the stone towers to make their homes.

The cat-like mammal, the fossa, can often be seen here hunting lemurs.

The limestone rocks are so sharp they can slice through clothes and flesh easily, making it very hard to climb or walk over them.

In the local language, tsingy means 'where one cannot walk barefoot'.

Von der Decken's sifaka

AFRICA

Fruit bat

Fossa

VALLÉE DE MAI NATURE RESERVE

The Vallée de Mai Nature Reserve is a lush palm forest on the island of Praslin in the Seychelles.

The Seychelles is a collection of 115 islands that lies 1,500 km east of mainland Africa.

Praslin island's remote location has helped it develop a unique range of palm trees and animals.

Praslin island is known for the coco de mer palm, which is also known as the sea coconut.

The fruit of the sea-coconut palm can reach 50 cm in diameter and weigh 30 kg.

It contains the largest seed in the whole plant kingdom. It often forms as a 'double' nut seed.

WOW!

The fruit takes six to seven years to mature and two more years to germinate.

There are five other palms that only grow here, including the brilliantly named Millionaire's Salad.

The nature reserve has a unique range of birds, mammals, crustaceans, snails and reptiles, like the tiger chameleon whose distinctive feature is a number of spikes on its chin!

The rare Seychelles black parrot can be found here — it loves eating the flowers of the coco de mer!

Coco de mer seed

AFRICA

Millionaire's Salad palm

Seychelles black parrot

EUROPE

1. St Kilda
2. Vatnajökull National Park
3. Norwegian Fjords
4. Danube Delta
5. Kvarken Archipelago
6. Mount Etna
7. Silfra Rift
8. Jurassic Coast
9. The Dolomites
10. Plitvice Lakes
11. Eisriesenwelt Ice Cave
12. Giant's Causeway
13. Wadden Sea
14. Aletsch Glacier
15. Primeval Beech Forests
16. Durmitor National Park
17. Western Caucasus
18. Doñana National Park
19. Virgin Komi Forests

Giant's Causeway

Doñana National Park

ST KILDA

St Kilda is a group of islands about 60 km west of Scotland's Outer Hebrides.

The largest island is called Hirta. It has the highest sea cliffs in the United Kingdom!

St Kilda is home to around 1 million seabirds.

COOL!

The islands have the largest colony of gannets in Europe with more than 60,000 pairs of birds.

The cliffs are a favourite breeding ground for puffins, with over 200,000 of the colourful birds nesting here.

The island of Soay has its own unique type of wild sheep, which is a very hardy and agile sheep that hides in the cliffs when scared.

No bees live on the islands but there are 140 species of beetles.

There are two animals that live only on these islands and nowhere else – the St Kilda wren and the St Kilda field mouse.

Stac an Armin is the tallest sea stack (a tall pillar of eroded rock that stands in the sea) in Britain. It stands at 196 m tall.

People lived on the islands until 1930 when the last residents left for the mainland.

Puffin

EUROPE

Soay wild sheep

Stac an Armin

VATNAJÖKULL NATIONAL PARK

In Vatnajökull National Park, Iceland, there are huge glaciers, ice caves, snowy mountains and bubbling hot springs.

The park covers 14% of Iceland, making it Europe's second largest national park.

The Vatnajökull ice cap is almost an entire kilometre thick in places.

WOW!

Vatnajökull is the largest glacier in Europe outside the Arctic with a surface area of 8,100 km².

The ice-covered peak of Hvannadalshnúkur is Iceland's highest mountain at 2,110 m.

There are several volcanoes under the ice cap. When these erupt they melt pockets of ice and cause big floods.

Around 30 individual glaciers flow out from the main Vatnajökull ice cap.

As glaciers retreat, water can fill the space they leave behind. This creates a glacial lake.

The largest glacial lake in Iceland is Jökulsárlón. It is up to 300 m deep and 25 km long.

Jökulsárlón glacial lake is dotted with floating icebergs. It has even featured in several movies!

Ice cave

EUROPE

Skaftafell glacier

Svartifoss waterfall

NORWEGIAN FJORDS

Norway's most iconic sight is its magnificent fjords, which often stretch inland for hundreds of kilometres.

Fjords are steep-sided valleys carved by huge glaciers.

As the glaciers melted, the huge chasms they had created were flooded by sea water.

The longest fjord in Norway is Sognefjord, known as 'the king of the fjords'. It runs inland for 205 km.

COOL!

Sognefjord is also the deepest fjord, with a maximum depth of 1,308 metres, meaning you could almost fit Ben Nevis — the UK's highest mountain — beneath the surface!

Cliffs in Sognefjord rise nearly sheer up from the water to 1,000 m high.

At the far end of Sognefjord is the Jostedalsbreen, continental Europe's largest glacier.

Nærøyfjord is the narrowest fjord. At one point it is only 250 m wide.

Nærøyfjord and Geirangerfjord have been rated by the National Geographic Society as the number one World Heritage site.

Many fjords have spectacular waterfalls. Geirangerfjord is known for the Seven Sisters waterfall, which is 410 m high.

EUROPE

DANUBE DELTA

The Danube Delta is the **best-preserved** natural river **delta** in Europe.

The delta is a haven for birds, with over 300 species spending the summer here.

The Danube Delta is the second-largest delta in Europe after the Volga Delta. It covers an area of 5,165 km² — about twice the size of the country of Luxembourg!

The Danube River flows for nearly 3,000 km through 9 countries on its way to the delta.

More than 1 million birds spend the winter in the delta.

Predator birds that live here include the osprey and the European eagle owl.

Mammals including the otter, mink and wildcat can all also be found on the prowl here.

The delta forms a huge labyrinth of streams, channels, lakes and ponds.

The waterways are rich in fish, with carp, tench, catfish, bream and the fearsome pike.

The delta is one of the least inhabited parts of Europe, giving the birds and animals plenty of peace and quiet!

Osprey

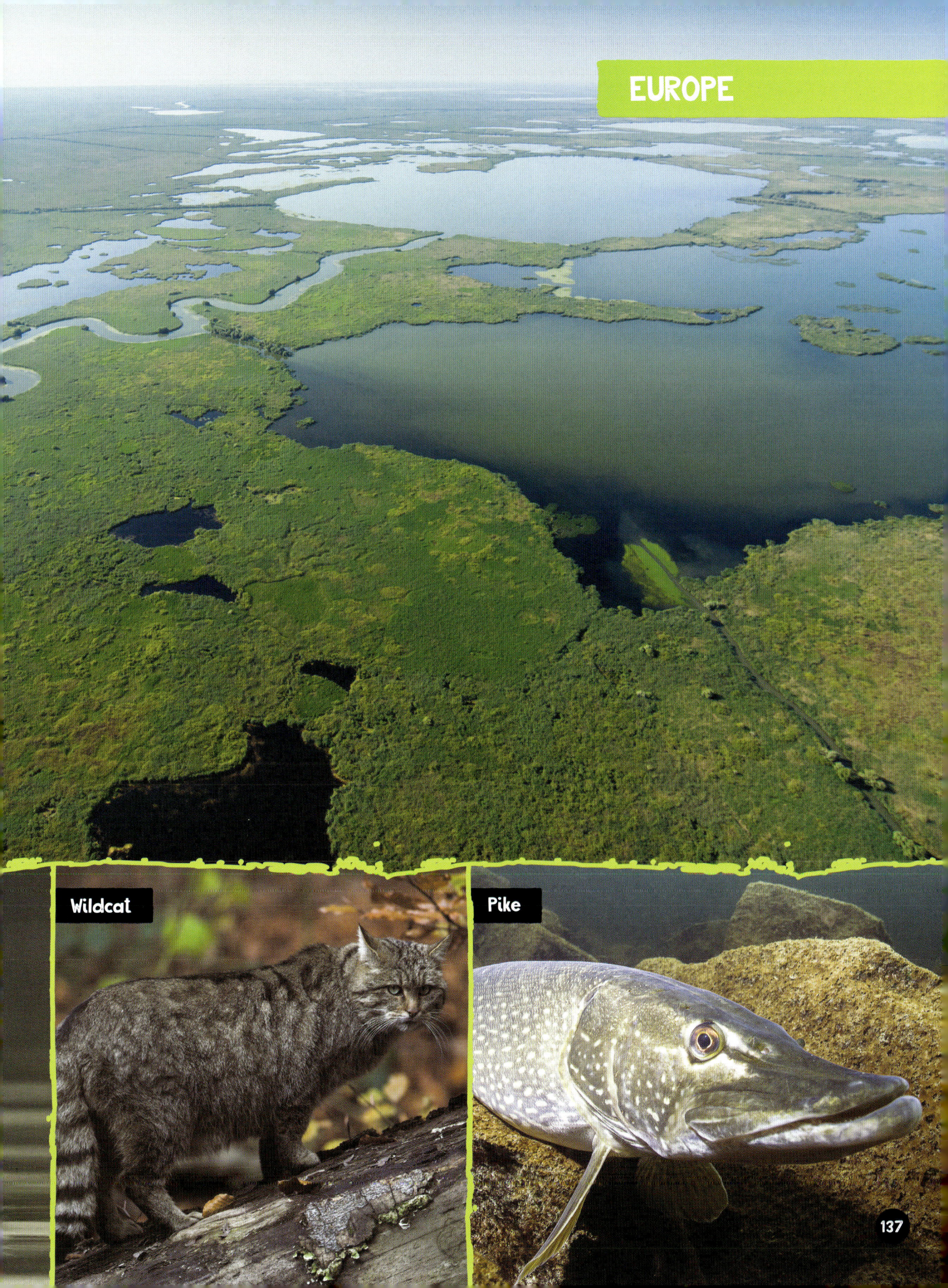

EUROPE

Wildcat

Pike

KVARKEN ARCHIPELAGO

The Kvarken Archipelago in Finland is a beautiful area of low-lying coastal islands where new land is being naturally created every year.

The Earth's crust was covered here by a huge glacial sheet in the last Ice Age.

As the weight of the ice has gone, the Earth's crust is now bouncing back up.

The islands and shoreline are rising up from the Gulf of Bothnia at a rate of 1 centimetre every year.

WOW!

The land is rising here faster than anywhere else in the world!

Many harbours in the area are now too far from the sea to be useful because of the rising land.

New islands are being created and older islands are growing in size.

Ringed seals and grey seals hunt for fish to eat in the waters around the islands.

Majestic-looking moose live on some of the larger islands. Moose like to swim! They can keep going for miles without stopping and even hold their breath underwater!

The shallow waters and rocks are perfect hunting grounds for birds like red-throated divers, black guillemots, cranes and buzzards.

Ringed seal

EUROPE

Moose

Red-throated diver

MOUNT ETNA

Mount Etna in Sicily, Italy, is one of the world's most active volcanoes.

Etna has erupted 10 times since 2000.

Most eruptions are at the top, where there are five separate craters.

Other eruptions happen on the sides of the mountain where there are more than 300 vents.

The vents range in size from small holes in the ground to huge craters hundreds of metres across.

An eruption in 2015 had a lava fountain 1 km tall and an ash plume that reached 3 km in height.

The base of Etna has a circumference of 140 km, making it by far the biggest of the three active volcanoes in Italy.

There are many orchards and vineyards around Etna, as the volcanic soil is great for growing plants.

On rare occasions the volcano puffs out perfect smoke rings!

Despite the heat of the volcano, there are two ski resorts on Mount Etna!

EUROPE

SILFRA
RIFT

Silfra is a rift in the surface of the Earth. The huge plates that hold North America and Europe together are moving apart here in western Iceland.

The pressure built up by the plates causes regular earthquakes.

The tectonic plates drift about 2 cm further apart every year.

The clear waters and steep sides of the rift make Silfra an amazing place to go scuba diving and snorkelling.

This is the only place in the world where you can dive directly between two continental plates. COOL!

'The Cathedral' here is a popular diving site. It's 100 m long and you can clearly see from one end to the other.

The water is clear but very cold (2–4°C), and you have to wear a dry suit to dive here.

Caves have formed in the rift by boulders falling into gaps.

The water in Silfra is meltwater from Langjökull, Iceland's second-largest glacier.

The water travels through porous underground lava to reach the rift – taking up to 100 years to make the journey!

EUROPE

JURASSIC COAST

The Jurassic Coast in England is a stretch of coastline known for its fossils.

The rocks here span 185 million years of geological history. COOL!

The Jurassic Coast is the only natural World Heritage site in England.

In different eras this area has been a desert, part of a tropical sea, and covered by swamps!

The fossils here have been studied by scientists for more than 200 years.

The fossil collector Mary Anning made many discoveries here. She was first to correctly identify an ichthyosaur and a plesiosaur.

Landslides often occur here, revealing fresh fossils in the layers of rock.

The Jurassic Coast is home to a fossil forest, made from trees that grew 140 million years ago in the Jurassic era.

One of the most common fossils you can find here are ammonites. These molluscs are closely related to today's octopus and squid.

Durdle Door is one of the coast's interesting rock formations. It is a natural arch of limestone, carved by wind and waves.

EUROPE

THE DOLOMITES

The Dolomites are a mountain range that form part of the Alps, but they have their own distinct character and colour.

Erosion of the mountains has created a spellbinding mix of spires, pinnacles, towers, sheer cliffs and crags.

There are 18 peaks over 3,000 m high.

Marmolada is the tallest peak at 3,343 m.

The Dolomites are made of a whitish rock and are also known as the 'Pale Mountains'.

Some of the cliffs are over 1,500 m high and are among the highest limestone walls found anywhere in the world.

Three main languages are spoken in the Dolomites: German, Italian and Ladin.

In 1991, an 'ice mummy' was found high in the mountains. The mummy was the 5,300-year-old body of a prehistoric man that had been well-preserved in solid ice.

WOW!

Animals living in the mountains include the chamois, brown bear, roe deer, fire salamander, marmot and Alpine newt—all adapted to life in cold and rugged conditions.

Fossils of sea creatures show that this massive mountain range was actually formed under the ocean 280 million years ago.

Chamois

EUROPE

Tre Cime di Lavaredo

Fire salamander

PLITVICE LAKES
NATIONAL PARK

Plitvice Lakes National Park in Croatia is famous for its stunning natural waterfalls that cascade into each other down different levels.

There are 16 lakes that are linked together in the cascade.

The lakes vary in colour from sky-blue to shades of green and grey.

WOW!

The different colours in the lakes are caused by minerals and micro-organisms in the water.

The lakes are separated from each other by natural terraces of travertine, a type of limestone.

The waterfalls drop a total of 133 m over 8 km.

The mountain slopes in the park are covered in dense forests of beech, spruce and fir trees.

The forests offer a perfect hunting ground for the grey wolf, eagle, owl, Eurasian lynx and European wildcat.

Brown bears can sometimes even be seen roaming through the woods. They dig out caves with their huge claws and sleep in them for most of the winter!

The park has over 300 different kinds of butterflies, including the striking Southern Festoon.

EUROPE

EISRIESENWELT
ICE CAVE

The Eisriesenwelt in Austria is the biggest ice cave in the world.

WOW!

Eisriesenwelt means 'World of the Ice Giants' in German.

The cave runs for over 40 km inside the Hochkogel mountain in the Austrian Alps.

Depsite its size though, only the first 1 km of the cave is open to tourists.

There is ice inside the cave even in summer. Cold wind blows out from the cave, keeping the temperature inside icy cold!

The cave passages were carved out of the mountain by a river.

The cave wasn't explored until the end of the 19th century. After Anton von Posselt-Czorich found it for the first time in 1879, it was forgotten about for many years!

Before the cave was explored, local people believed that it was an entrance to hell.

The cave ice is formed by water seeping down through cracks in the rock into the freezing caverns.

There are thousands of caves in the Alps but only a few are filled with ice like this one.

EUROPE

GIANT'S CAUSEWAY

Sea pinks

The Giant's Causeway in Northern Ireland is made of geometric rock columns formed by volcanic activity 60 million years ago.

There are more than 40,000 interlocking columns.

WOW!

The columns were formed when molten lava flooded to the Earth's surface.

As the lava cooled it formed regular shapes.

Most of the pillars are hexagonal, although some have four, five, seven or eight sides.

The columns range from 38–51 cm in diameter and stand up to 28 m high.

Some of the column formations have earnt nicknames! These include 'the camel's humps', 'the chimneys' and the 'eyes of the giants'.

The beautiful cliffs, seashores, marshes and grasslands are home to 50 species of birds and more than 200 species of plants, like sea pinks.

Seabirds that live here include the fulmar, petrel, cormorant, shag, redshank, guillemot and razorbill.

The Giant's Causeway is named after the mythological Irish giant Finn MacCool, who is said to have challenged the Scottish giant Benandonner to a fight and built the causeway to reach him.

EUROPE

Giant interlocking columns

Razorbill

WADDEN SEA

In between the land of northwest Europe and the low Frisian islands is an eerie, empty world of mudflats, creeks and sandbanks—the Wadden Sea.

Wadden is thought to come from the Frisian and Dutch word 'wad', which means 'mud flat'.

The Wadden Sea stretches along 500 km of coastline.

The large German rivers Elbe, Weser and Ems all drain into the Wadden Sea.

The coast by the Wadden Sea is vulnerable to flooding, and bad floods often change the shape of the coastline.

Tides and currents shift sand and mud around the sea. The islands of Vlieland and Ameland have even moved eastwards through the centuries! WOW!

The Wadden Sea is an important habitat for harbour seals and grey seals. Grey seals tend to be less shy and much more curious than harbour seals!

Harbour porpoises and white-beaked dolphins also swim in the deeper waters.

Atlantic salmon and brown trout used to swim in the Wadden Sea, but have now sadly disappeared.

The mudflats, creeks and sandbars are visited by 10 million birds in spring and autumn — the greatest number of migratory birds in Europe.

Grey seal pup

EUROPE

Oystercatcher

White-beaked dolphin

ALETSCH GLACIER

The Aletsch Glacier in Switzerland is the mightiest iceflow in the Alps.

The glacer is 23 km long and covers an area of 81 km² — about twice the area covered by the city of Cambridge!

It is also up to 1 km thick.

The glacier is formed by four smaller glaciers flowing into one.

The 11 billion tonnes of ice in the glacier scours the Alpine valleys it flows down, breaking off rocks and scraping away at slopes.

The Aletsch Glacier flows down its mountain channel at a rate of 200 m every year.

If the Aletsch Glacier melted, it could give every person on Earth 1 litre of water every day for 4½ years!

WOW!

Meltwater from the glacier forms the Massa River which then feeds into the Rhône River.

Like most glaciers in the world today, the Aletsch Glacier is a retreating glacier, meaning that since 1980 it has lost 1.3 km of its length.

11,000 years ago, the glacier extended all the way down into the Rhône river valley, but today it doesn't reach anywhere near that far.

PRIMEVAL BEECH FORESTS

The Carpathian Mountains have some of the last remaining intact virgin forests in the whole of Europe. These are forests that have remained largely untouched since they first grew.

Beech trees are adaptable and their forests expanded across Europe after the last Ice Age 12,000 years ago.

Beech forests once covered large areas of continental Europe. Today these beautiful forests only exist in isolated areas.

UNESCO has grouped together 78 forests in 12 European countries to give them protected status.

There are protected areas in Albania, Belgium, Bulgaria, Germany, Italy, Croatia, Austria, Romania, the Slovak Republic, Slovenia, Spain and Ukraine.

The trees provide a habitat for organisms such as mushrooms, moss, lichen and insects.

Rare birds such as the capercaillie and black grouse live in the forests. Capercaillies make a noise like a bouncing ping-pong ball when they are trying to attract a mate!

Bats, brown bears, wolves and lynxes are all at home in the woods too.

In the Białowieża Forest in Poland there are 800 European bison, the heaviest wild land animal in Europe.

WOW!

The **European bison** is also known as the **wisent** or the **zubr**. Males eat over **30 kg of food** every day!

Capercaillie

EUROPE

European bison

Black grouse

DURMITOR
NATIONAL PARK

The glacier-carved mountains of Durmitor in Montenegro are covered in dense forest and studded with crystal-clear lakes.

There are about 50 peaks over 2,000 m high, which rise above alpine meadows and forests.

The Tara River Canyon here is the deepest gorge in Europe at 1,300 m deep. WOW!

The Tara Canyon has sandy beaches, high cliffs, and more than 80 large caves to explore.

The mountain landscape is dotted with 18 glacial lakes, which local people call 'mountain eyes'.

There are many subterranean rivers — rivers that are formed from glacial lakes seeping underground.

Black Lake (in the picture) is the best-known glacial lake. In summer a narrow part of the lake dries up, creating two separate lakes.

There are some magnificent wild mammals in the park, including the brown bear, grey wolf and European wildcat.

Over 100 species of birds have been seen here, including the golden and short-toed eagle, honey buzzard, peregrine falcon and capercaillie.

The peregrine falcon is the fastest bird and animal on the planet. It can swoop down to catch prey at speeds of over 300 km/h!

EUROPE

WESTERN CAUCASUS

The Caucasus mountain range runs for 1,200 km from the Black Sea to Baku on the Caspian Sea.

The mountain range creates a natural border between Europe and Asia.

Mount Elbrus is the highest peak in Europe at 5,642 metres above sea level.

Mount Elbrus is also an inactive volcano – it last erupted over 2,000 years ago.

It is also the highest point in the world that a vehicle has ever managed to get to. Alexander Abramov drove a Land Rover up there on a 43-day journey!

The Western Caucasus is the only large mountain area in Europe that has not been changed by humans. COOL!

The Persian leopard, a rare large cat, is being reintroduced in the area. They are generally nocturnal animals that hunt for prey like goats and wild boar at night.

There is a grove of 85 m high Nordmann Fir that are thought to be the tallest trees in Europe.

The dense forests on the lower mountain slopes are home to the wolf, bear, lynx and wild boar.

The endangered European bison is now happily living in these wild mountain lands.

Mountain goats

EUROPE

Persian leopard

Wild boar

DOÑANA
NATIONAL PARK

Iberian lynx

Doñana National Park in southern Spain is an important wetland reserve for birds and rare wildlife.

The coastline, marshes and sand dunes make up the largest nature reserve in Europe.

Doñana lies close to the Strait of Gibraltar, which separates Europe and Africa. It is the perfect 'stop off' for migrating birds!

Some of Doñana's sand dunes move around the reserve over time. These 'mobile dunes' have their own unique ecosystem.

To avoid being buried in moving sand, trees like the Sea Juniper coil their roots up so that they 'float' while the sand is moving, and then uncoil them when it's stopped moving so that they can anchor them again! COOL!

Many types of turtles live here, like the loggerhead and leatherback turtles.

The endangered Iberian lynx still survives in the park. This beautiful feline has become a symbol of the reserve.

Flamingos create a 'pink carpet' when they come to feed and breed at the park!

In the winter more than 500,000 waterfowl come here to enjoy the warm temperatures and plentiful food.

One of the world's rarest eagles, the Spanish imperial eagle, can often be seen hunting here.

EUROPE

Flamingo

Spanish imperial eagle

VIRGIN
KOMI FORESTS

The Virgin Komi Forests are the largest old forests in Europe.

The forests cover an area of 32,800 km² – that's almost the size of Denmark!

The forests lie in the Komi Republic, which is part of Russia.

The Komi Forests lie in the northern Ural Mountains.

The Urals separate Europe from Asia and extend for 2,400 km.

The Komi Forests are part of the taiga – a cool landscape of pine, spruce and larches that is also known as 'snow forest'.

COOL!

Taiga has only existed for around 12,000 years. Before this the land here lay under a vast ice sheet.

As well as millions of trees, the Komi Forests contain peat bogs, rivers and beautiful lakes.

Bears, wolves, reindeer, lynxes and otters all live here. Lynxes are particularly well-adapted to life in the snow, with their very thick fur and huge paws with retractable claws that stop them from sinking into the snow!

Eagles, buzzards and many other birds of prey soar above the trees.

Otter

EUROPE

Taiga

Reindeer

MIDDLE EAST & ASIA

1. The Dead Sea
2. Lut Desert
3. Kali Gandaki Gorge
4. Pamukkale
5. Volcanoes of Kamchatka
6. Ha Long Bay
7. Rainbow Mountains
8. Wulingyuan
9. Lake Baikal
10. Hang Sơn Đoòng
11. Sichuan Giant Panda Sanctuaries
12. Great Himalayan National Park
13. The Sundarbans
14. Yakushima Island
15. Lorentz National Park
16. Red Beach
17. Lena Pillars
18. Kazakh Steppe
19. Ujung Kulon National Park
20. Nanda Devi and The Valley of Flowers

Pamukkale

Great Himalayan National Park

THE DEAD SEA

The shore of the Dead Sea, in the Jordan Rift Valley in the Middle East, is 434 metres below sea level.

The sea is the lowest point on Earth's surface.

The Dead Sea is a 'hypersaline lake' – a very salty body of water cut off from the ocean.

The Dead Sea is nearly 10 times saltier than the ocean. WOW!

The sea's saltiness makes swimming in it feel like you're always floating!

At 304 m deep, it is the deepest hypersaline lake in the world.

It is so salty that no plants, fish, or any other creatures can survive there.

Many animals live in the mountains surrounding the Dead Sea, including ibex, hyraxes, jackals, leopards and hundreds of bird species.

The Dead Sea is shrinking. In 1930 its surface area was 1,050 km^2 but today it is just 605 km^2.

The Dead Sea was one of the world's first health resorts – people have bathed in its salty waters for thousands of years to get the benefit of its healing properties.

Hyrax

MIDDLE EAST & ASIA

Salt deposits

Jackal

LUT DESERT

The Lut Desert, located in Iran, is an exceptionally dry and hot salt desert, surrounded by mountains.

The desert is known as 'Dasht-e Lut' in Persian which means 'Emptiness Plain'.

A NASA satellite found the desert is the hottest land surface on Earth, with its sand reaching a temperature of over 70°C. WOW!

In the spring wet season a little water flows from the mountains, but it soon dries up completely leaving only sand, salt and bare rocks.

Kaluts are impressive rock towers carved by sand and wind over thousands of years.

In the centre of the desert the wind has carved the kaluts into ridges and furrows. These stretch for over 150 km and can be 75 m tall.

There is a sea of sand or 'erg' in the southeast of the desert.

The sand dunes in the erg are over 475 m high, making them among the tallest in the world.

In some places the wind has stripped away all sand and soil, leaving stony desert pavements called 'hamada'.

More than half of the desert is covered in volcanic rocks.

MIDDLE EAST & ASIA

KALI GANDAKI GORGE

Kali Gandaki Gorge is the world's deepest gorge.

This huge canyon plunges down over 5,500 m between two neighbouring mountains.

The gorge lies in the Himalayas, the highest mountain range in the world.

The gorge lies between the seventh highest and the tenth highest mountains in the world. *COOL!*

The Dhaulagiri mountain (8,167 m high) is on the west side of the gorge and Annapurna (8,091 m high) is on the east.

The Gandaki River that runs through the gorge rises on the border between Tibet and Nepal.

The Gandaki River has 1,025 glaciers feeding into it.

The river is a good place to find fossilised shells.

The gorge was cut by a river that is older than the surrounding mountains.

As the Himalayas were pushed upwards over millions of years, the river continued cutting its way through the uplifting earth.

MIDDLE EAST & ASIA

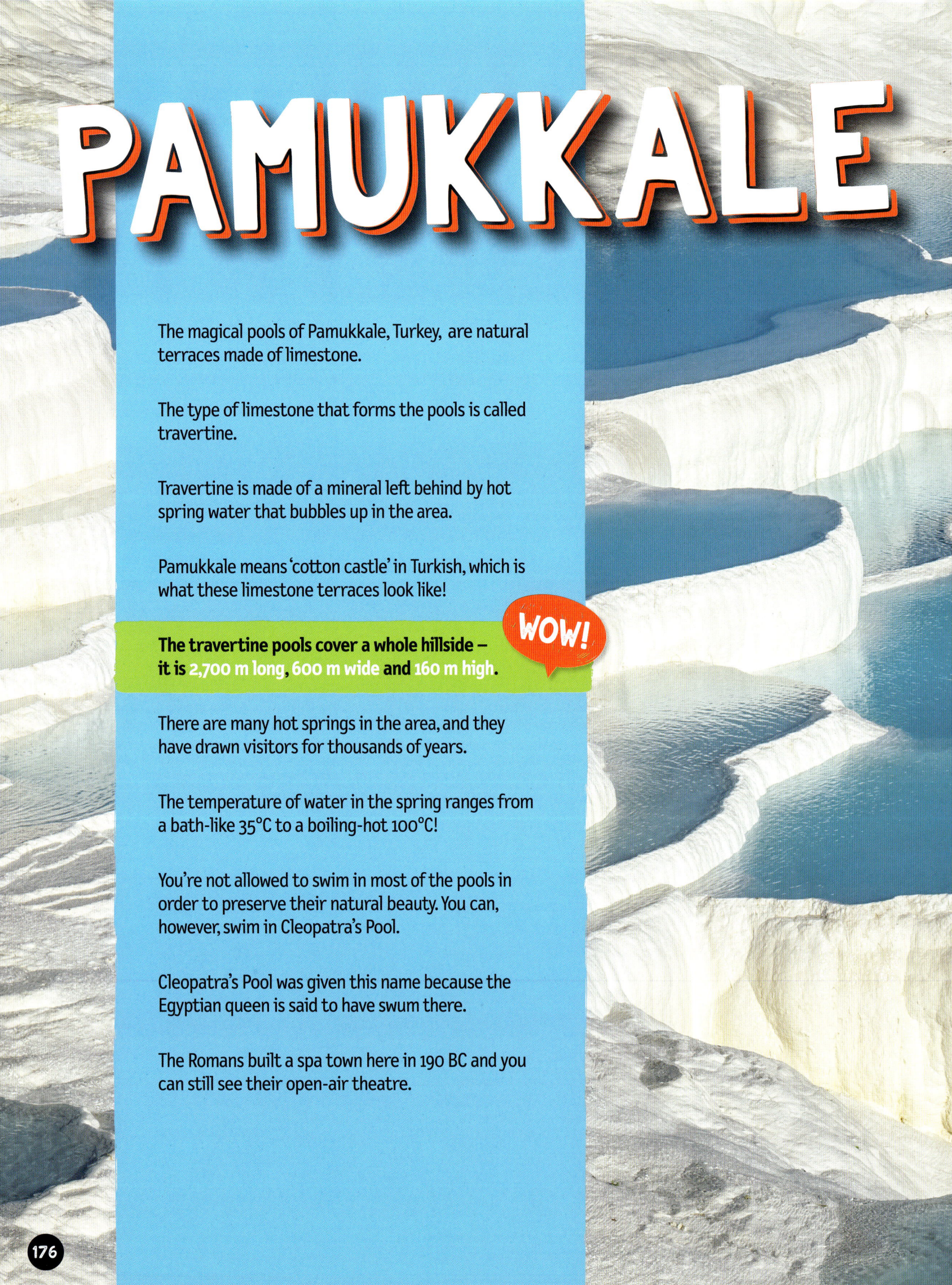

PAMUKKALE

The magical pools of Pamukkale, Turkey, are natural terraces made of limestone.

The type of limestone that forms the pools is called travertine.

Travertine is made of a mineral left behind by hot spring water that bubbles up in the area.

Pamukkale means 'cotton castle' in Turkish, which is what these limestone terraces look like!

The travertine pools cover a whole hillside – it is 2,700 m long, 600 m wide and 160 m high. WOW!

There are many hot springs in the area, and they have drawn visitors for thousands of years.

The temperature of water in the spring ranges from a bath-like 35°C to a boiling-hot 100°C!

You're not allowed to swim in most of the pools in order to preserve their natural beauty. You can, however, swim in Cleopatra's Pool.

Cleopatra's Pool was given this name because the Egyptian queen is said to have swum there.

The Romans built a spa town here in 190 BC and you can still see their open-air theatre.

MIDDLE EAST & ASIA

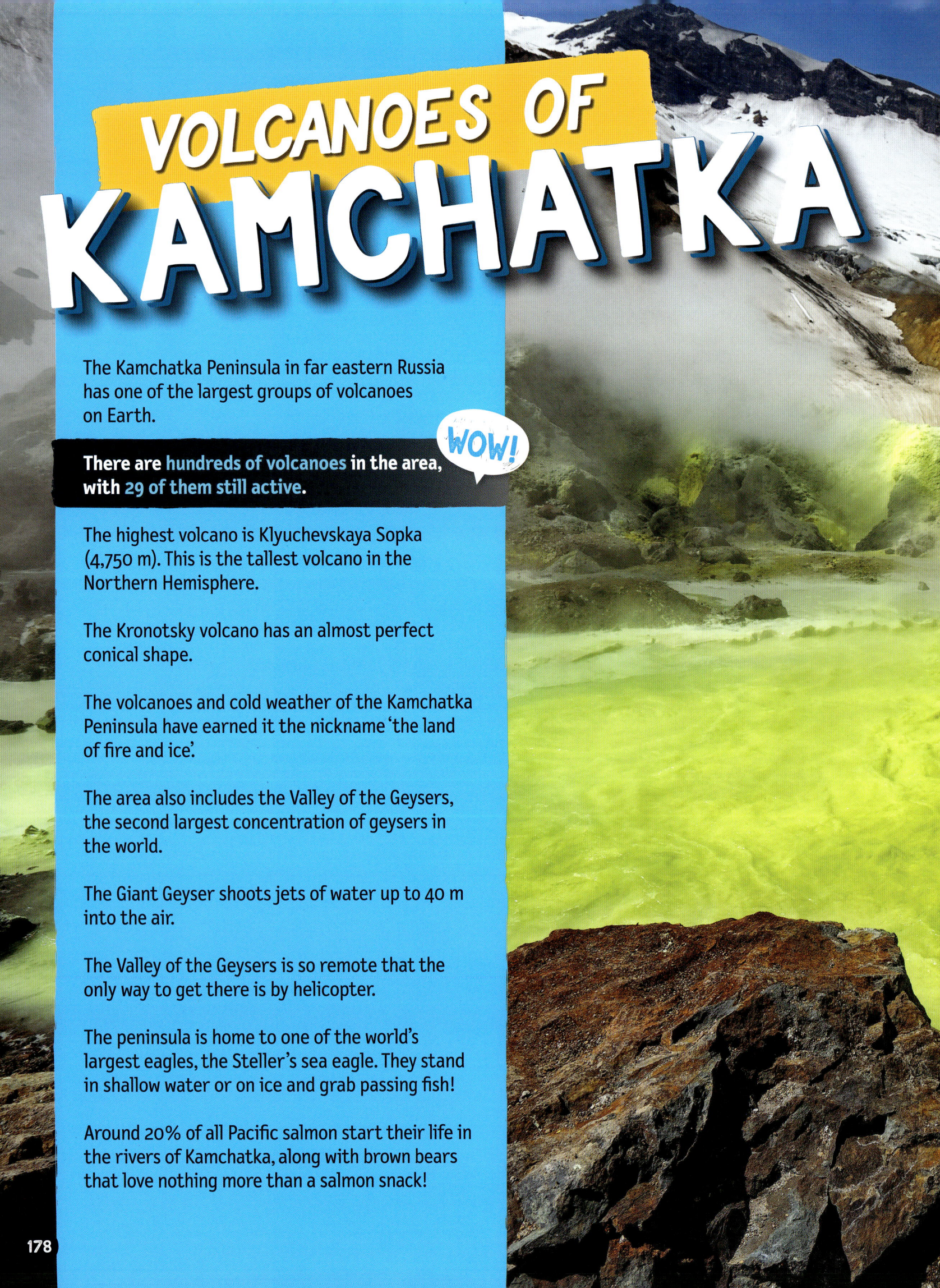

VOLCANOES OF KAMCHATKA

The Kamchatka Peninsula in far eastern Russia has one of the largest groups of volcanoes on Earth.

There are hundreds of volcanoes in the area, with 29 of them still active. WOW!

The highest volcano is Klyuchevskaya Sopka (4,750 m). This is the tallest volcano in the Northern Hemisphere.

The Kronotsky volcano has an almost perfect conical shape.

The volcanoes and cold weather of the Kamchatka Peninsula have earned it the nickname 'the land of fire and ice'.

The area also includes the Valley of the Geysers, the second largest concentration of geysers in the world.

The Giant Geyser shoots jets of water up to 40 m into the air.

The Valley of the Geysers is so remote that the only way to get there is by helicopter.

The peninsula is home to one of the world's largest eagles, the Steller's sea eagle. They stand in shallow water or on ice and grab passing fish!

Around 20% of all Pacific salmon start their life in the rivers of Kamchatka, along with brown bears that love nothing more than a salmon snack!

MIDDLE EAST & ASIA

HA LONG BAY

Ha Long Bay in Vietnam has thousands of small islands sticking up from the sea in remarkable shapes.

Ha Long means 'descending dragon'.

COOL!

There are over 2,000 islands in the bay.

The islands are made of limestone, which is easily shaped by water. These structures are called karsts.

Many of the islands are hollow and have large caves inside.

During the war between America and Vietnam, a big cave in the bay was used as a safe house and hospital for injured soldiers.

Most of the islands have dense forest growing on top.

One of the rarest primates in the world, the white-headed langur, has found a safe home in the forests of the bay's islands.

The bay is rich in marine life, and sea eagles can often be seen catching their food.

Many floating villages exist and thrive in Ha Long Bay.

Karst

MIDDLE EAST & ASIA

White-headed langur

Cave in Ha Long Bay

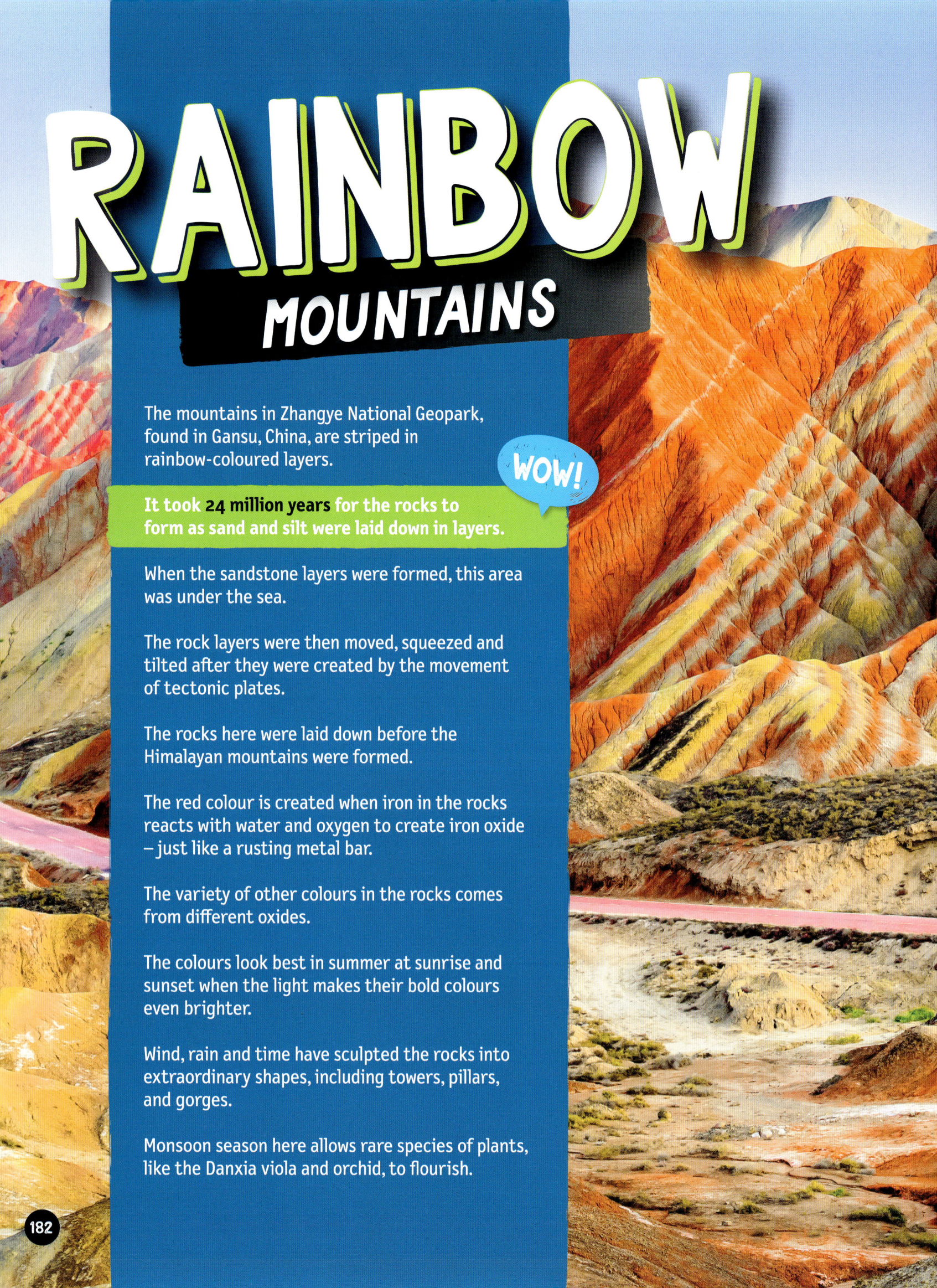

RAINBOW MOUNTAINS

The mountains in Zhangye National Geopark, found in Gansu, China, are striped in rainbow-coloured layers.

It took 24 million years for the rocks to form as sand and silt were laid down in layers.

When the sandstone layers were formed, this area was under the sea.

The rock layers were then moved, squeezed and tilted after they were created by the movement of tectonic plates.

The rocks here were laid down before the Himalayan mountains were formed.

The red colour is created when iron in the rocks reacts with water and oxygen to create iron oxide – just like a rusting metal bar.

The variety of other colours in the rocks comes from different oxides.

The colours look best in summer at sunrise and sunset when the light makes their bold colours even brighter.

Wind, rain and time have sculpted the rocks into extraordinary shapes, including towers, pillars, and gorges.

Monsoon season here allows rare species of plants, like the Danxia viola and orchid, to flourish.

MIDDLE EAST & ASIA

WULINGYUAN

Wulingyuan in Hunan, China, has an extraordinary mountain landscape of towering rock pillars, forests, streams, pools and waterfalls.

The pillars are the remains of a sandstone mountain that has been eroded over time.

The rock of the mountains here was formed 400 million years ago.

The highest rock pillar is 1,262 m tall, making it taller than Snowdon (the highest mountain in Wales).

There are more than 40 caves with cool calcite crystals in the mountains.

After rainstorms, the mountains can be covered in a mysterious sea of fog (like in the picture).

Two of the rock structures are **connected** by one of the **highest natural bridges** in the world – Tianqiashengkong – which means 'bridge across the sky'.

COOL!

The site is home to lots of vulnerable animals, like the dhole (a kind of wild dog), the Asiatic black bear, and the Chinese water deer.

Most of the rock pillars are topped with trees and plants, where you can also see a variety of impressive birds, like the red-billed blue magpie.

The mountains inspired the scenery of the planet Pandora in the film *Avatar*.

MIDDLE EAST & ASIA

LAKE BAIKAL

Lake Baikal is the largest freshwater lake in the world, spanning Mongolia and Russia. It holds around one-fifth of all fresh water on Earth.

Baikal's surface area is larger than Belgium!

It is the oldest lake in the world, and has existed for over 25 million years.

Baikal is also the deepest lake in the world at 1,642 m.

The lake contains more water than the Five Great Lakes of North America put together! WOW!

There are many islands on the lake. Most of them don't have any people living on them, but Olkhon, the biggest island, is home to about 1,700 people!

More than 1,000 species of plants and 2,500 species of animals live in or around the lake. The Baikal seal, that is only found here, is the only species of seal that lives in fresh water.

The lands around the lake are home to the brown bear, wolf, elk, reindeer and wild boar — animals that can all withstand the freezing, harsh conditions here.

In winter, the ice on the lake can be 2 m thick.

Lake Baikal is one of the clearest bodies of water in the world. On a clear day, you can see 40 metres into the lake!

Baikal seals

MIDDLE EAST & ASIA

Brown bear

Thick ice

HANG SO'N ĐOÒNG

Hang So'n Đoòng, near the Laos–Vietnam border, is the largest natural cave in the world.

The cave is 200 m high and runs for over 9 km.

Hang So'n Đoòng means 'cave of the mountain river'.

Some stalagmites (mounds of salt deposits rising from the cave's floor) in the cave are 70 m tall.

The cave is so big that a Boeing 747 plane could fly through the cave without its wings being in any danger of hitting the sides. WOW!

Some woodlice, fish and millipedes that live inside the cave in complete darkness are completely white.

The cave was first discovered in 2009 by three British divers who were exploring the network of waterways and tunnels in the area.

The three million-year-old cave has its own subterranean (underground) river.

The roof has collapsed in two places in the cave letting sunlight in. This means that forests can grow in the light.

The main cavern has its own climate – clouds sometimes form in it.

MIDDLE EAST & ASIA

SICHUAN GIANT PANDA SANCTUARIES

The Sichuan Giant Panda Sanctuaries in China are home to more than 30% of the world's pandas.

WOW!

The sanctuaries have the largest natural area for giant pandas in the world.

Pandas are very vulnerable and there are only around 1,800 pandas left living in the wild.

Other globally endangered animals such as the red panda, the snow leopard and clouded leopard also have a safe home here.

The forests that the sanctuaries are in have more unusual plant life than any place on Earth outside tropical rainforests.

There are around 6,000 species of plants and trees here.

Bamboo shoots and leaves make up 99% of a panda's diet.

Pandas' forepaws have five fingers and a thumb which helps them grip bamboo.

A panda can eat up to 14 kg of bamboo a day.

A panda poos around 40 times a day! And the rest of their time is spent eating or sleeping!

Giant panda

MIDDLE EAST & ASIA

Bamboo

Red panda

GREAT HIMALAYAN NATIONAL PARK

The Great Himalayan National Park in India is a protected part of the Himalayan mountains.

The Himalayas is a very large mountain range that contains many of the world's highest peaks.

The range has nine out of ten of the world's highest mountains.

Many rivers start in the park and the thick forests keep the water clean for the people on the Indian plains downriver.

The lowest point in the national park is at 1,500 m. The highest is at 6,000 m.

The range of altitudes in the park allow very different species to flourish.

Lofty spruce trees grow high up, while in the lower valleys, horse chestnut trees grow.

There are some amazing animals here, including the very rare snow leopard.

Snow leopards have really long tails — these can be used to keep them warm, but also as fat storage for times when it's tricky to find food.

Snow leopards also use their tails to help them balance when stalking prey. They creep up on their prey from above and then chase them down a slope, making 6-metre-high jumps!

COOL!

Himalayan mountains

MIDDLE EAST & ASIA

Snow leopard

Himalayan forests

THE SUNDARBANS

The Sundarbans mangrove forest, spanning India and Bangladesh, is a maze of tidal waterways, mudflats and small islands that covers 10,000 km^2 – an area half the size of Wales.

Sundarban means 'beautiful forest' in Bengali.

The forest is in the Ganges River Delta. A delta is the flat, broad area where the river meets the sea.

A mangrove is an area of shrubs and small trees growing in salty or muddy sea water.

The Ganges is 2,525 km long and the third-largest river on Earth. It is sacred to Hindus.

The Sundarbans provide a safe home for Bengal tigers as well as many birds, spotted deer, crocodiles and snakes.

Tigers are good swimmers, and they swim among the mangrove islands to hunt deer.

COOL!

Other wild cats in the Sundarbans include the jungle cat, fishing cat and leopard cat.

The Sundarbans also protect millions of people against floods caused by cyclones – huge tropical storms.

Mangrove swamps are found in tropical and subtropical parts of the world.

Bengal tiger

MIDDLE EAST & ASIA

Spotted deer

Fishing cat

YAKUSHIMA ISLAND

Yakushima Island in Japan has a fantastical landscape of mountains, waterfalls and ancient forests.

Yakushima is famous for its unspoiled forests.

The magical moss-covered forests are known for their giant Japanese cedar trees.

One of the island's most famous trees is known as Jōmon Sugi. At over 25 m, this cypress tree is the largest conifer in Japan.

Jōmon Sugi is an ancient tree; although its exact age is unknown, it's thought it could be up to 7,200 years old.

COOL!

Visitors to the island can bathe in one of its many natural hot springs.

Hot springs here can reach 48°C!

The centre of the island has a range of steep mountains almost 2,000 m high — Yakushima is sometimes referred to as the 'Alps of the Ocean'.

The annual rainfall on the island is 8,000 mm — that's 14 times as much rain as London gets!

The island has its own unique species of monkey — the red-bottomed macaque, which has, unsurprisingly, been named after the colour of its bottom!

Yakushima deer

MIDDLE EAST & ASIA

Japanese cedar trees

Red-bottomed macaques

LORENTZ
NATIONAL PARK

Cassowary

WOW!

The **Lorentz National Park** in New Guinea has the **biggest variety** of **unusual plants** and **animals** of almost any place on the planet.

Lorentz covers an area of 25,056 km², making it the largest national park in southeast Asia.

It has marine areas, mangroves, tidal and freshwater swamp forest, lowland and montane rainforest, and even alpine tundra and equatorial glaciers.

At the peak of the park is Puncak Jaya, which at 4,884 m high is the tallest mountain between the Himalayas and the Andes.

The dingiso is a species of tree-kangaroo that only lives on this island. It was discovered in 1994.

Two species of cassowary, a big flightless bird, live in the park. If provoked, they can produce a dangerous kick!

A very unusual rodent lives in the mountains here— the huge alpine woolly rat.

Two species of echidna thrive here. Echidnas are one of only two mammals that lay eggs (the other is the platypus).

Quolls, possums and wallabies are all marsupials (mammals with pouches) that roam the forests here.

Lorentz Park has many unmapped and unexplored areas, which will certainly have plants and animals yet unknown to science!

MIDDLE EAST & ASIA

Short-beaked echidna

Quoll

RED BEACH

At Red Beach in Panjin, China, shallow seas wash against shores that are brilliant shades of red.

The bright red colour comes from an unusual type of seaweed that grows here. COOL!

Chemicals in the soil mean that the red seaweed is one of the few plants that can grow here.

The seaweed starts growing in April when it is pinkish. Later in the year it turns deep red.

The beach area at Panjin is the largest reed marsh in the world.

Only a small part of the huge wetland area can be visited by tourists.

More than 260 kinds of birds and almost 400 kinds of wild animals live in the marshes.

One of the rarest cranes (a type of bird) in the world, the red-crowned crane, breeds here. The beach is often nicknamed 'home of the cranes'!

The red-crowned crane is a symbol of luck and long life.

The beach is the largest breeding area for the endangered black-mouth gull.

MIDDLE EAST & ASIA

LENA PILLARS

The Lena Pillars are narrow rocky towers that line the banks of the Lena River in far east Siberia.

At 4,400 km long, the Lena is the eleventh-longest river in the world, and the longest river in Russia.

The Lena Pillars range from 150–300 m high.

The pillars form sheer cliffs that run for 40 km along the river bank.

WOW!

The pillars are made of layers of rock that have been eroded by weather and natural forces.

Deep gullies form when water freezes in cracks in the rock and shatters it.

Meltwater carves the gullies deeper after frost has shattered rock.

In winter the temperature here can reach an icy −60°C!

The nearest city to the pillars is Yakutsk, the coldest city in the world.

The area is also excellent for fossil hunting, with many unique discoveries made here.

MIDDLE EAST & ASIA

KAZAKH STEPPE

The Kazakh Steppe is a huge area of open grassland in northern Kazakhstan and parts of Russia.

The steppe stretches for more than 2,200 km across Asia.

This is the largest dry steppe region on Earth, covering approximately 804,450 km^2 – an area larger than Turkey!

Wildlife on the Kazak steppe includes marmots, wolves and the endangered saiga antelope.

Towards the south, the steppe is mostly desert.

In the north, there are pine groves mixed with open grasslands.

The endangered steppe tortoise lives in the grasslands. They can spend up to nine months a year being completely inactive! WOW!

There are wetlands and lakes in the Saryarka area of the northern steppe.

More than 15 million birds visit the wetlands of the northern steppe every year.

The wetlands are home to the world's most northerly group of pink flamingos.

Steppe wolf

MIDDLE EAST & ASIA

Saiga antelope

Steppe tortoise

UJUNG KULON
NATIONAL PARK

Ujung Kulon National Park is a peninsula of rainforest that reaches into the Indian Ocean and offers a haven for some very special creatures.

The park contains the largest lowland rainforest in Java.

Ujung Kulon is the last refuge for the critically endangered Javan rhinoceros.

There are only around 60 Javan rhinos left in the wild.

There are three primates that only live in the forests here – the Javan gibbon, Javan leaf monkey and silvered leaf monkey.

Unusual mammals in the rainforest include the leopard, wild dog, leopard cat, fishing cat, Javan mongoose and several species of civets.

Despite civets sometimes being called 'civet cats', they are actually much more closely related to mongooses than cats!

The park is close to the volcano Krakatoa, which exploded in one of the biggest eruptions in history in 1883.

The 1883 Krakatoa explosion produced a tsunami that hit the island of Krakatoa and surrounding areas, and covered the entire area in a thick layer of ash.

WOW!

The volcanic eruption caused all humans to flee the area, leaving the animals and plants to live on undisturbed.

Javan rhinoceros

MIDDLE EAST & ASIA

Krakatoa

Javan gibbon

NANDA DEVI AND THE VALLEY OF FLOWERS

The gentle slopes of the Valley of Flowers and the rugged mountain wilderness of Nanda Devi together form a breathtaking landscape on the edge of the Himalayas.

Nanda Devi is a stunning lone peak that stands 7,817 m high and is one of the steepest mountains in the world.

The Valley of Flowers is known for its meadows of blooms with orchids, poppies, primulas, marigolds, daisies and anemones carpeting the ground.

COOL!

The Valley of Flowers is 8 km long, 2 km wide and runs to 3,658 m above sea level.

The area is remote and hard to get to. As a result, both areas were unexplored until the 1930s.

The Valley of Flowers was actually discovered by accident in 1931 by three mountaineers who got lost on their way back from a climb!

Nanda Devi is a sacred mountain. To respect this, and to preserve its fragile ecosystem, the peak has been closed to climbers since 1983.

Rare animals enjoy the quietness here, including the Asiatic black bear, musk deer and snow leopard.

Scientists have counted 498 types of flowers in the valley, and many of them grow nowhere else on Earth.

You need a permit to visit the Valley of Flowers and overnight stays are forbidden to help preserve the valley's beauty.

Asiatic black bear

MIDDLE EAST & ASIA

Nanda Devi

Musk deer

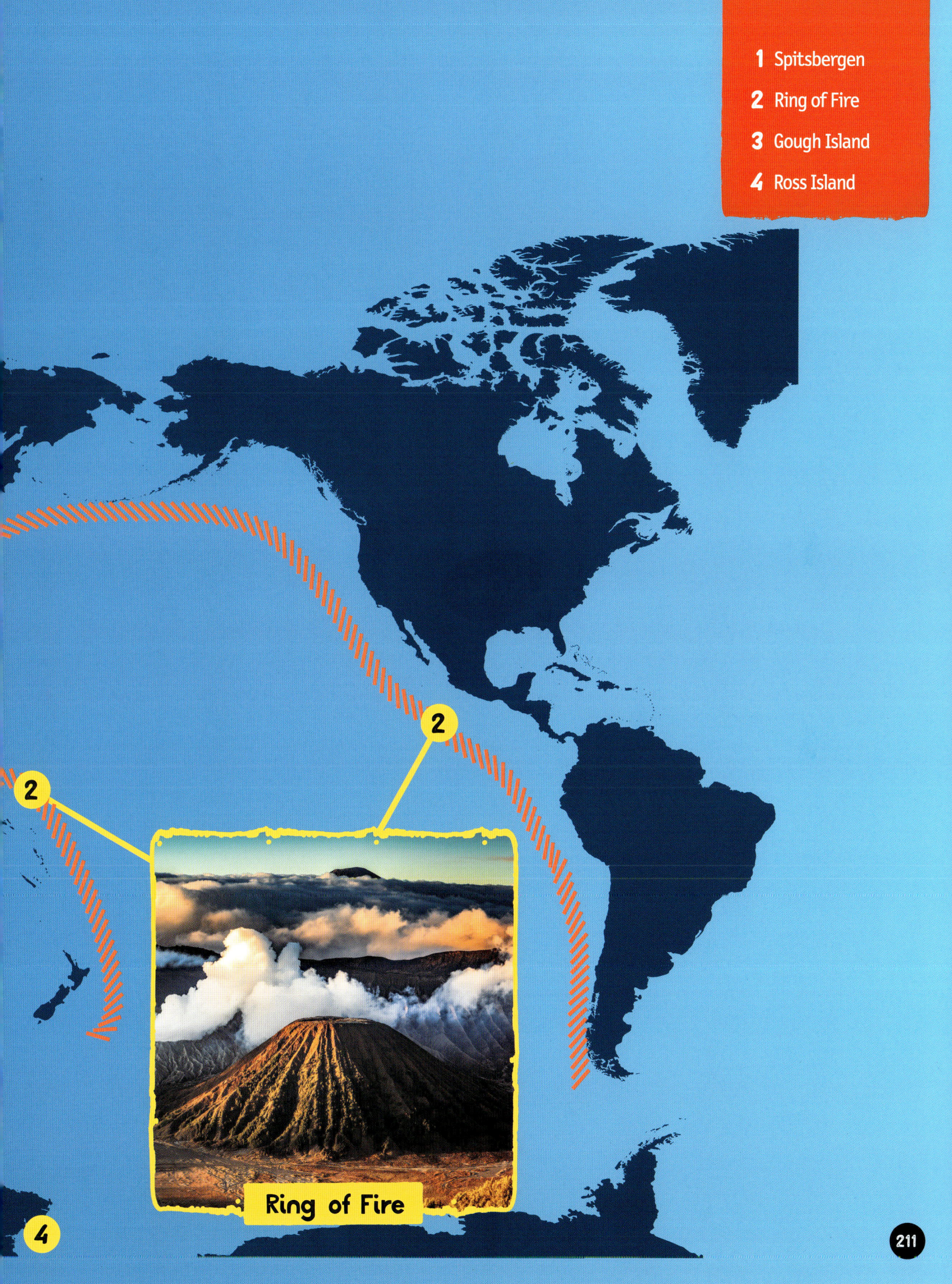

1 Spitsbergen
2 Ring of Fire
3 Gough Island
4 Ross Island

Ring of Fire

SPITSBERGEN

Deep in Svalbard, in the Arctic Circle, lies the island of Spitsbergen, where polar bears roam wild and the midnight sun shines.

There are six protected national parks on Spitsbergen.

It's thought that around 270 polar bears live on Spitsbergen and the surrounding Svalbard islands.

Polar bears often hunt by waiting at a seal's breathing hole, ready for dinner to pop up!

WOW!

Every spring more than three million seabirds — like little auks — visit the area.

The island is so far north that in the summer, the sun never sets — this is known as the 'midnight sun'.

For much of the winter, the sun never rises above the horizon and the island is in complete darkness.

Reindeer are plentiful on the island — their very thick coats help them survive the cold temperatures.

Walruses can often be seen on the beaches and icefloes around the island.

They use their long tusks for fighting and to dig holes in the ice.

Polar bear

ISLANDS & OCEANS

Walrus

Reindeer

RING OF FIRE

The Ring of Fire is an area around the Pacific Ocean with a large number of volcanoes.

It is at least 35 million years old.

The Ring of Fire forms a horseshoe that goes up the east side of Asia and Oceania and down the west side of the Americas.

The Ring is 40,000 km long and up to 500 km wide.

There are 450 active volcanoes in the Ring of Fire, 75% of Earth's total number of active volcanoes. WOW!

The volcanic activity is caused by the movement of tectonic plates against each other.

The four largest volcanic eruptions on Earth in the last 11,700 years happened in the Ring of Fire.

The Ring contains the world's highest active volcano – Ojos del Salado in the Andes which is 6,893 m high.

90% of the world's earthquakes also happen here.

The largest volcanic explosion in human history took place in the Ring of Fire – at Tambora in Indonesia in 1815. The explosion was heard over 2,500 km away!

ISLANDS & OCEANS

GOUGH ISLAND

Gough Island is a rocky and remote outcrop in the middle of the South Atlantic Ocean.

Gough is one of the remotest islands in the world. It is over **3,200 km** from South America and about **400 km** from the nearest island.

COOL!

Gough Island has spectacular sea cliffs that are nearly 500 m high.

There are no people living on Gough Island, apart from a few scientists who spend time working at the island's weather station.

Gough's remoteness means that it has one of the most undisturbed ecosystems on Earth.

The island is home to almost the entire world population of the endangered Tristan albatross.

There are also between 30,000 and 65,000 pairs of rockhopper penguins on the island. Rockhoppers have distinctive spiky black and yellow feathers on their heads!

Southern right whales cruise the waters around the island.

Fur seals bask on the rocks and shores of the island. Fur seals are well adapted to survive cooler temperatures with their thick fur, but if they get too hot in summer they have to take mudbaths to cool down!

There is a problem with house mice eating bird eggs on the island — the mice escaped from ships during the 19th century!

Tristan albatross

ISLANDS & OCEANS

Southern right whale

Rockhopper penguin

ROSS ISLAND

Ross Island is a frozen, barren island near Antarctica that is made up of four volcanoes.

Mount Erebus is the only active volcano on the island. Mount Terror, Mount Bird and Mount Terra Nova are inactive.

Mount Erebus is the planet's southernmost active volcano. It is 3,794 m high. WOW!

Mount Erebus has been active for over 1 million years and has a lava lake near its peak.

The Mount Erebus and Mount Terror volcanoes were named after the ships commanded by Sir James Clark Ross, the explorer who discovered the island.

Although it is quite small, Ross Island is the world's highest island on average.

It is also the most southerly island reachable by sea. Many explorers used it as their base for expeditions to Antarctica.

Ross Island looks like it is part of Antarctica because it is almost completely surrounded by the Ross Ice Shelf, a huge plate of ice that floats on the ocean.

The Ross Ice Shelf is about the size of France and is several hundred metres thick.

The largest iceberg in history split from the Ross Ice Shelf in 2000. Iceberg B-15 was 295 km long, 37 km wide and 11,000 km² in area – larger than Jamaica!

ISLANDS & OCEANS

GLOSSARY

archipelago: a group of islands.

atoll: a ring-shaped coral reef or island.

canyon: a narrow valley between hills or mountains, often with a river running through it. See also: **gorge**.

cyclone: a huge tropical storm with very strong winds and often accompanied by heavy rainfall.

delta: a wide area of land made from sand and soil dropped by slow-moving rivers.

dormant (volcano): an active volcano that hasn't erupted recently, but could erupt again in the future.

dry season: a regular period of time when it remains almost constantly dry.

canyon

ecosystem: a community of living organisms that interact and/or depend on each other in a certain environment.

equator: the imaginary line that runs all the way around Earth, dividing the northern hemisphere (top half) from the southern hemisphere (bottom half).

erosion: when something like a rock or coastline is gradually worn away, usually by wind or water.

fjord: a steep-sided valley carved by huge glaciers.

fumarole: an opening in Earth's crust that spews out steam and volcanic gases.

geyser: a large spurt from the Earth's crust of hot water and steam. The water is heated underground by magma.

glacier: a mass of ice that is slowly moving. It is formed from ice, snow, rock, sediment and sometimes liquid water, on land, and moves slowly down a slope due to gravity and its weight.

global warming: the gradual increase in temperature of the planet due to human actions, like burning fossil fuels.

gorge: a narrow valley between hills or mountains. A gorge usually has steep walls or cliffs either side, and a river running through it. See also: **canyon**.

isthmus: a narrow strip of land connecting two bigger areas of land. The strip of land has sea on both sides.

GLOSSARY

lagoon: a small lake or pool.

lava: hot, liquid rock that erupts from a volcano.

magma: the incredibly hot material deep beneath the Earth's surface.

mangrove: an area of shrubs and small trees growing in salty or muddy sea water.

meltwater: water formed from snow and ice melting.

migration: when animals move from one area to another at a certain time of year.

monolith: a huge single rock standing on its own.

peninsula: a piece of land that sticks out into water.

plateau: an area of level high ground.

rift (valley): an area (or valley) where tectonic plates are being pulled apart.

salt flat: an area of flat land coated with salt as a result of evaporated water.

savannah: a large grassy plain.

sea stack: a tall pillar of eroded rock that stands in the sea.

sinkhole: a hole that forms when water dissolves surface rock.

stalactite: mineral deposits that grow from the ceiling downwards, typically in a cave.

stalagmite: mineral deposits that grow from the ground upwards, typically in a cave.

subterranean river: a river running underground.

supercontinent: a huge area of land bigger than several countries.

supervolcano: a huge volcano that could cause serious damage if it erupted.

tectonic plate: the vast rocky areas of the Earth's crust that are constantly moving.

tidal bore: a huge wave that forms when the spring tide is constricted as it enters a long, narrow, shallow inlet.

tsunami: a massive sea wave that is usually caused by an earthquake. Tsunamis often cause mass destruction and devastation.

volcanically active: an area that contains volcanoes that have erupted recently and are likely to erupt again soon.

wetland: land that is very wet and consists of marshes and swamps.

wet season: a regular period of time where it rains almost constantly.

sea stack

INDEX

A

Africa 96–127, 164
African golden cat 116
Albania 158
Alberta 82
Aldabra Atoll 114
alligator 70
Alps, the 146, 150, 156
Amazon rainforest 40
Ameland 154
anaconda 46, 48
Andean mountain cat 50, 52
Andes 28, 30, 40, 50, 52, 198, 214
Angel Falls 36
Annapurna 174
Antarctica 218
anteater 32, 40
antelope 112, 122, 204
Arctic Circle 212
Argentina 32, 34
Arizona 66, 74
armadillo 52
Asia 162, 166, 168–209, 214
Atlantic Ocean 38, 44, 48, 216
Atol das Rocas 44
atoll 44, 114
Australia 8, 12, 16, 18, 24
Austria 150, 158
aye-aye 110
Ayers Rock 12

B

badlands 82
Baku 162
bamboo 190
Bangladesh 194
Barringer Crater 66
bat 12, 22, 64, 124, 158
bear 50, 68, 72, 76, 78, 84, 146, 148, 158, 160, 162, 166, 178, 184, 186, 208, 212
beaver 68
bee 124, 130
beetle 60, 76, 108, 130
Belgium 158, 186
Belize 58
Benin 112
Białowieża Forest 158
bison 72, 158, 162
Black Lake 160
Black Sea 162
bobcat 76, 84
Bolivia 28, 46
Botswana 122
Brazil 32, 38, 46, 48
Brazilian Atlantic Islands 44

Bridalveil Fall 84
buffalo 20, 100, 112, 122
Bulgaria 158
Burkina Faso 112
bushbaby 98
butterfly 46, 86, 148
buzzard 100, 138, 160, 166
Bwindi Impenetrable Forest 116

C

caiman 32, 46
California 62, 84, 88
Canada 68, 78, 82, 86, 90
Canaima National Park 36
Caño Cristales 40
canyon 72, 74, 90, 124, 160, 174
capybara 52
caribou 68
Carlsbad Caverns National Park 92
Carpathian Mountains 158
Caspian Sea 162
Caucasus mountain range 162
cave 12, 56, 58, 68, 92, 132, 142, 148, 150, 160, 180, 184, 188
Cave of Crystals 56
Challenger Deep 10
chameleon 124, 126
chamois 146
Charles Darwin 42
cheetah 100, 104
chimpanzee 116, 120
China 182, 184, 190, 200
chipmunk 76
civet 206
Cleopatra's Pool 176
cliff 16, 68, 82, 84, 130, 134, 146, 152, 160, 202, 216
coco de mer 126
cololco 50
Colombia 40, 48
condor 50, 74
coprolite 82
coral reef 8, 44, 58, 94, 114
Cordillera Blanca 50
Costa Rica 60
cougar 34, 40, 84
Cousteau, Jacques 58
coyote 74, 76, 78, 84
crab 114
crane 138, 200
crater 22, 64, 66, 140
Crater Lake 22
Croatia 148, 158
crocodile 24, 32, 70, 102, 104, 122, 194
crystals 56, 84, 184

D

Dallol volcano 118
Danakil Depression 118
Dasht-e Lut 172
Dead Sea, the 170
Deadvlei 108
deer 20, 46, 70, 76, 84, 146, 184, 194, 196, 208
delta 122, 136, 194
delta, Danube 136
delta, Ganges river 194
delta, Okavango 122
delta, Volga 136
Democratic Republic of the Congo 120
desert 30, 62, 102, 144, 172, 204
Devils Hole Pupfish 62
Dhaulagiri 174
dhole 184
dingiso 198
dingo 24
Dinosaur Provincial Park 82
dive site 8, 44, 58, 142, 188
Dolomites, The 146
dolphin 16, 44, 68, 88, 154
Dolphin Bay 44
Doñana National Park 164
dragonfly 64
dry season 38, 40, 48
dugong 8, 16
Durdle Door 144
Durmitor National Park 160

E

eagle 20, 32, 78, 100, 110, 148, 160, 164, 166, 178, 180
earthquake 142, 214
echidna 18, 198
ecosystem 8, 40, 70, 74, 82, 164, 208, 216
Ecuador 42
Egypt 102
Eisriesenwelt ice cave 150
El Capitan 84
elephant 98, 100, 112, 122
elk 76, 186
endangered species 8, 38, 40, 52, 60, 64, 70, 88, 104, 110, 116, 120, 162, 164, 184, 190, 200, 204, 206, 216
England 144
equator 42, 50
erosion 58, 66, 82, 92, 130, 146, 172, 182, 184, 202
Erta Ale 118
eruption 22, 64, 72, 132, 140, 206, 214
Ethiopia 118
Europe 128–167
Everglades National Park 70

F

falcon 74, 84, 100, 160
fern, King 24
Fernando de Noronha 44
film 10, 22, 28, 132, 184
Finland 138
Finn MacCool 152
firefly 76
fish 8, 10, 16, 38, 40, 44, 46, 48, 58, 62, 72, 88, 122, 136, 138, 178, 188, 194, 206
fishing cat 194, 206
fjord 14, 68, 80, 134
flamingo 106, 164, 204
flooding 46, 58, 100, 122, 132, 134, 154, 194
Florida 70
fog 30, 108, 184
forest 14, 18, 24, 32, 34, 36, 40, 52, 60, 64, 76, 86, 94, 98, 110, 112, 116, 120, 126, 144, 148, 158, 160, 162, 166, 180, 184, 188, 190, 192, 194, 196, 198, 206
fossa 124
fossil 16, 74, 82, 90, 102, 144, 146, 174, 202
fox 68, 84, 102
Franchetti Island 118
Fraser Island 24
frazil ice 84
Frisian islands 154
fumarole 94

G

Gaet'ale Pond 118
Galápagos Islands 42
Gansu 182
Geirangerfjord 134
Germany 158
geyser 72, 178
Giant Geyser, the 178
Giant's Causeway 152
gibbon 206
Gibraltar 164
giraffe 98, 100, 104
glacial lake 50, 132, 160
glacier 14, 34, 50, 68, 78, 80, 84, 90, 98, 132, 134, 142, 156, 174, 198
global warming 8, 34, 80
gold prospectors 62
Gondwana Rainforests 18
gorge 74, 100, 160, 174, 182
gorilla 116, 120
Gough Island 216
Grand Canyon National Park 74
Grand Prismatic Pool 72
grasslands 46, 50, 98, 152, 204
Great Barrier Reef 8
Great Blue Hole 58
Great Himalayan National Park 192
Great Smoky Mountains National Park 76
Greenland 80

INDEX

Gros Morne National Park 68
guanaco 34
Gulf of Bothnia 138
Gulf of California 88
gypsum 56, 92

H

Ha Long Bay 180
Hang Son Đoòng 188
hare 68, 78
harsh conditions 28, 30, 62, 68, 78, 106, 118, 170, 186, 212
Hawaii 64
Hawaii Volcanoes National Park 64
Himalayas 174, 182, 192, 198, 208
hippopotamus 112
Hirta 130
Hochkogel mountain 150
hot spring 72, 118, 132, 176, 196
Huascarán National Park 50
hummingbird 30, 60
Hunan 184
Hvannadalshnúkur 132
hyrax 170

I

ibex 170
ibis 38
ice 34, 62, 84, 98, 132, 138, 146, 150, 156, 166, 178, 186, 212, 218
Ice Age 58, 68, 84, 90, 138, 158
iceberg 80, 132, 218
ice cave 34, 132, 150
icefjord 80
Iceland 132, 142
ice mummy 146
Idaho 72
Iguaçu Falls 32
Iguaçu National Park 32
Ilulissat Icefjord 80
India 192, 194
Indian Ocean 16, 114, 206
Indonesia 20, 214
insects 12, 30, 38, 40, 64, 112, 158
invasive species 70
Iran 172
Isla Ángel de la Guarda 88
Isla Marajó 48
island 8, 14, 16, 20, 22, 24, 32, 42, 44, 48, 60, 64, 88, 94, 110, 114, 118, 126, 130, 138, 154, 180, 186, 194, 196, 198, 206, 212, 216, 218
Isla Tiburón 88
Italy 140, 158

J

jackal 102, 170
jaguar 32, 40, 52, 60
jaguarundi 60
Japan 196
Java 206

Jimmie Angel 36
Jökulsárlón 132
Jōmon Sugi 196
Jordan Rift Valley 170
Jostedalsbreen 134
jungle cat 194
Jurassic Coast 144

K

Kali Gandaki Gorge 174
Kamchatka Peninsula 178
kangaroo 18, 198
karst 180
Kazakhstan 204
Kazakh Steppe 204
Kīlauea 64
Kilimanjaro National Park 98
kiwi 14, 22
Kluane, Wrangell–St Elias and Glacier Bay park 78
Klyuchevskaya Sopka 178
koala 18
Komi Republic 166
komodo dragon 20
Komodo National Park 20
Krakatoa 206
Kronotsky 178
Kvarken Archipelago 138

L

lagoon 38, 44, 114, 122
lake 14, 22, 24, 38, 50, 62, 72, 106, 118, 132, 136, 148, 160, 166, 170, 186, 204, 218
Lake Afrera 118
Lake Baikal 186
Lake Natron 106
Langjökull 142
langur 180
Laos 188
lava 64, 94, 118, 140, 142, 152, 218
Lechuguilla Cave 92
lemur 110, 124
Lena Pillars 202
Lençóis Maranhenses National Park 38
leopard 98, 100, 104, 122, 162, 170, 190, 192, 206, 208
leopard cat 194, 206
Lesser Sunda Islands 20
limestone 58, 92, 124, 144, 146, 148, 176, 180
lion 74, 100, 104, 112, 122
lizard 20, 42, 44
llama 34
Lorentz National Park 198
Los Glaciares National Park 34
Lut Desert 172
lynx 68, 78, 148, 158, 162, 164, 166

M

macaque 20, 196
Mackenzie Mountains 90

Madagascar 110, 124
manatee 38, 70
mangrove 44, 70, 194, 198
Manu National Park 52
margay 60
Mariana trench 10
marine iguana 42
Marmolada 146
marmot 78, 84, 146, 204
marsh 70, 108, 152, 164, 200
Mary Anning 144
Mauna Loa 64
meltwater 142, 156, 202
meteorite crater 66
Mexico 56, 86
Middle East 170
midnight sun 212
migration 86, 104, 154, 164
migratory birds 154, 164
Mikeno 120
Milford Sound 14
Millionaire's Salad 126
millipede 188
minerals 36, 56, 72, 92, 148, 176
mink 136
mist 36, 84, 90, 100, 108
Monarch Butterfly Biosphere Reserve 86
Mongolia 186
mongoose 102, 206
monkey 40, 60, 98, 116, 196, 206
monolith 12
monsoon 182
Montana 72
Montenegro 160
moonbow 100
moose 68, 138
mountain 14, 28, 30, 34, 36, 40, 44, 50, 52, 60, 68, 72, 74, 76, 78, 90, 94, 98, 116, 120, 132, 140, 146, 148, 150, 156, 158, 160, 162, 166, 170, 172, 174, 182, 184, 188, 192, 196, 198, 208
Mount Bird 218
Mount Cook (Aoraki) 14
Mount Doom 22
Mount Elbrus 162
Mount Erebus 218
Mount Etna 140
Mount Everest 10
Mount Fitz Roy 34
Mount Kilimanjaro 98
Mount Logan 78
Mount Ngauruhoe 22
Mount Ruapehu 22
Mount Stanley 120
Mount Terra Nova 218
Mount Terror 218
Mount Tongariro 22
mouse 18, 130, 216
mudflat 154, 194
mummy 146

N

Nærøyfjord 134
Nahanni National Park 90
Namibia 108
Namib-Naukluft Park 108
Nanda Devi and The Valley of Flowers 208
NASA 30, 172
national park 14, 20, 22, 32, 34, 36, 38, 42, 50, 52, 64, 68, 70, 72, 74, 76, 84, 90, 92, 98, 104, 116, 120, 132, 148, 160, 164, 192, 198, 206, 212
native tribe 12, 52
Nepal 174
New Guinea 198
New Mexico 92
newt 146
New Zealand 14, 22
Ngauruhoe 22
Niagara Falls 90, 100
Niger 112
Noronha skink 44
North America 54–95, 142, 214
Northern Ireland 152
North Island, New Zealand 22
North pole 78
Norwegian fjords 134

O

Oceania 6–25, 214
ocelot 36, 60
octopus 144
Ojos del Salado 214
Old Faithful 72
Olkhon 186
oncilla 38
orca 68, 88
orchid 36, 90, 182, 208
osprey 136
otter 32, 38, 46, 52, 68, 136, 166
Outer Hebrides 130
owl 74, 110, 122, 136, 148

P

Pacific Ocean 10, 30, 214
Pale Mountains 146
Pamukkale 176
Panama 60
panda 190
Panjin 200
Pantanal, the 46
panther 70
Paraguay 46
penguin 42, 216
peregrine falcon 84, 100, 160
Peru 48, 50
Pitons, the 94
platypus 198
playa 28
Plitvice Lakes National Park 148

223

Poland 158
Pororoca 48
porpoise 68, 88, 154
possum 12, 18, 198
prairies 82
Praslin 126
prehistoric man 146
primate 180, 206
Primeval Beech Forests 158
puma 34, 36, 50, 52, 60
Puncak Jaya 198

Q

Queen of the Andes 50
Queensland 24
quoll 198

R

raccoon 76
rain 28, 30, 38, 46, 58, 62, 76, 86, 110, 122, 182, 184, 196
rainbow 40, 100
Rainbow Mountains 182
rainforest 14, 18, 24, 36, 40, 110, 198, 206
Rainforests of the Atsinanana 110
rat 110, 124, 198
ray 16, 88, 102
Red Beach 200
reef 8, 44, 58, 92, 94, 114
reindeer 166, 186, 212
rhinoceros 104, 122, 206
Ring of Fire 214
River, Amazon 48, 52
River, Awash 118
River, Colorado 74
River, Danube 136
River, Elbe 154
River, Ems 154
River, Gandaki 174
River, Ganges 194
River, Iguaçu 32
River, Lena 202
River, Madre de Dios 52
River, Manu 52
River, Massa 156
River, Nile 48
River, Okavango 122
River, Rhône 156
River, South Nahanni 90
River, subterranean 160, 188
River, Tara 160
River, Weser 154
River, Zambezi 100
rock 12, 40, 62, 68, 74, 82, 84, 92, 124, 130, 144, 152, 156, 172, 182, 184, 202, 216
Romania 158
Ross Ice Shelf 218
Ross Island 218
Ruapehu 22
Russia 166, 178, 186, 202, 204

S

Saint Lucia 94
salamander 76, 146
Salar de Uyuni 28
salt flat 28, 62
salt lake 118
sand dune 24, 38, 62, 102, 108, 164, 172
sandstone 12, 112, 182, 184
satellite 28, 172
savannah 40, 112
scientists 8, 42, 52, 56, 74, 80, 92, 118, 144, 208, 216
Scotland 130
seabird 42, 88, 130, 152, 212
sea coconut 126
seal 68, 138, 154, 186, 212, 216
sea lion 78
Sea of Cortés 88
sea snake 8, 20, 102
sea stack 68, 130
sequoia, giant 84
Serengeti National Park 104
Seven Sisters waterfall 134
Seychelles 126
shark 16, 24, 44, 58, 102
Shark Bay 16
Siberia 202
Sichuan Giant Panda Sanctuaries 190
Sicily 140
sifaka 124
Silfra Rift 142
sinkhole 58
skeleton 102, 118
skunk 76
Slovak Republic 158
Slovenia 158
snake 8, 20, 46, 70, 82, 194
Soay 130
Sognefjord 134
South America 26–53, 60, 214, 216
South Atlantic Ocean 44, 48, 216
South Island, New Zealand 14
South pole 78
Spain 158, 164
Spitsbergen 212
squid 88, 144
squirrel 68, 74
Stac an Armin 130
stalactite 92
stalagmite 92, 188
St Kilda 130
Strait of Gibraltar 164
stromatolite 16
sugar glider 18
Sundarbans, The 194
sunrise 182
sunset 12, 84, 182
supercontinent 18
supervolcano 72
Svalbard 212
swamp 144, 194, 198
Switzerland 156

T

Tablelands 68
table-top mountain 36
taiga 166
Talamanca range 60
Tambora 214
Tanzania 98, 104, 106
tapir 60
Tara canyon 160
tectonic plates 10, 18, 68, 106, 118, 142, 182, 214
Te Wahipounamu 14
Tibet 174
tiger 194
toad 30
Tongariro National Park 22
tortoise 42, 114, 204
tourists 34, 74, 150, 200
travertine 148, 176
Tsingy de Bemaraha Strict Nature Reserve 124
tsunami 206
Turkey 176
turtle 8, 16, 44, 48, 88, 94, 102, 164

U

Uganda 116
Ujung Kulon National Park 206
Ukraine 158
Uluru 12
United Kingdom 130
United States 70, 76
Ural Mountains 166

V

Vallée de Mai Nature Reserve 126
Valley of Flowers 208
Valley of the Geysers 178
vaquita 88
Vatnajökull National Park 132
Venezuela 36
Victoria Falls 100
Vietnam 180, 188
Virginia Falls 90
Virgin Komi Forests 166
Virunga National Park 120
Vlieland 154
volcano 22, 42, 44, 64, 72, 94, 98, 118, 120, 132, 140, 162, 178, 206, 214, 218
Volcanoes of Kamchatka 178
Vredefort crater 66
vulture 112

W

Wadden Sea 154
Wadi Al-Hitan, 102
wallaby 12, 18, 198
walrus 212
W-Arly-Pendjari 112
warthog 98
waterfall 14, 32, 36, 64, 68, 84, 100, 132, 134, 148, 184, 196
waterway 70, 136, 188, 194
Western Brook Pond 68
Western Caucasus 162
wetlands 46, 112, 122, 164, 200, 204
wet season 40, 48, 110, 172
whale 44, 68, 78, 80, 88, 94, 102, 216
whale shark 16, 94
Whale Valley 102
wild boar 162, 186
wildcat 102, 136, 148, 160
wild dog 112, 184, 206
wildebeest 104
wind 38, 62, 82, 102, 144, 150, 172, 182
wolf 78, 104, 148, 158, 160, 162, 166, 186, 204
wolverine 78
wombat 18
Wulingyuan 184
Wyoming 72

Y

Yakushima Island 196
Yakutsk 202
Yellowstone National Park 72
Yosemite National Park 84

Z

Zambia 100
zebra 98, 100, 104
Zhangye National Geopark 182
Zimbabwe 100

IMAGE CREDITS

All images © Shutterstock.com except the following images: pp.10–11: all images ©NOAA Office of Ocean Exploration and Research, https://oceanexplorer.noaa.gov; pp.48–49: main image © JACQUES JANGOUX / SCIENCE PHOTO LIBRARY; pp.56–57: © JAVIER TRUEBA / MSF / SCIENCE PHOTO LIBRARY; p.65: Hawaiian hoary bat © Nature Picture Library / Alamy Stock Photo; p.89: Humboldt squid © robertharding / Alamy Stock Photo; pp.208–209: main image © HIRA PUNJABI / Alamy Stock Photo